Donated by Ryan White
2003

THE SHELL

Five Hundred Million Years of Inspired Design

THE

Five Hundred Million Years

SHELL

of Inspired Design

BY **HUGH** and **MARGUERITE STIX**

AND **R. TUCKER ABBOTT**

Du Pont Chair of Malacology, Delaware Museum of Natural History

PHOTOGRAPHS BY **H. LANDSHOFF**

Abradale Press
Harry N. Abrams, Inc., Publishers, New York

Library of Congress Cataloging-in-Publication Data
Stix, Hugh.
    The shell: five hundred million years of inspired design/by
Hugh and Marguerite Stix and R. Tucker Abbott; photographs
by H. Landshoff.
        p.   cm.
    Bibliography: p. 313
    Includes index.
    ISBN 0–8109–8087–8
    1. Shells–Pictorial works. I. Stix, Marguerite. II. Abbott, R.
Tucker (Robert Tucker), 1919–   . III. Landshoff, Herman, 1905–
IV. Title.
QL404.S7 1988
594′.0471–dc19   88–6384
                                                              CIP

This 1988 edition is published by Harry N. Abrams, Inc., New York

A Times Mirror Company

Printed and bound in Japan

CONTENTS

INTRODUCTION

Shells and Man

Shells as an Economic Factor

A Religious Symbol

Pre-Columbian America

The Middle Ages—St. James and the Scallop Shell

Heraldry

The Renaissance

The Late Renaissance and the Baroque

The Eighteenth Century—Rococo

The Victorian Approach

The Emerging Science of Malacology

The Shell in the Twentieth Century

PLATES

BIBLIOGRAPHY OF MARINE SHELLS

INDEX OF ILLUSTRATED SHELLS

INTRODUCTION

All beginnings are difficult; it was necessary, we thought, to find a completely new approach to man's fascination with shells (a powerful force in early societies). Throughout all parts of the world, excavations have yielded evidence of man's early and continuing attachment to the shell, both as a cult symbol and as an aesthetic object. Religion, art, and sorcery have found inspiration in the shell or in its representation.

Following the Victorian era, an age of extravagant romanticizing, interest in the shell went into a sharp decline, particularly in the United States, where infatuations tend to be violent and short-lived. The serious collector remained on the scene, but he was a rare exception in a world now largely taken over by children encouraged by weary parents who saw in the shell a perfect source of organized, stimulating play. The person who collected solely for the sake of collecting, however, continued to pursue his aims as usual, nursing a passion that could just as well have been satisfied by matchbook covers, tea cozies, or old telephones.

We wanted to change this attitude, to restore some of the admiring awe man had experienced throughout history for the work of these strange sea creatures, master builders whose architectural miracles embodied the bases of a multitude of mathematically correct vaults, arches, staircases, porticoes, and niches. We wanted to direct attention to a world of ideas that might give fresh meaning and stimulation to the contemporary arts—to free-form creation, sculpture, architecture, design—especially to those areas where confusion and darkness seem to prevail.

We ran at once into a wall of disbelief. Well-meaning friends who had supported our ideas throughout a lifetime thought we had become senile overnight. "Seashells? *Really*?" We were seriously advised to pool our considerable energies and put them into something more worthwhile and more tangible. One friend even said flatly, "Shell, hell!" dismissing the whole subject as not worth discussing. It became obvious to us that something drastic was needed to wipe out long-standing prejudices. It was then that we decided we would search the world for the most beautiful and glamorous shells we could find and exhibit them in a simple but elegant way as objects deserving attention and respect.

The first stop in our journey was Tokyo, capital of a nation whose people have always considered shell collecting among the most venerable of traditions. We realized the strength and importance of the word "venerable" in the mind of a Japanese on the first day of our visit, when we hired a driver to taxi us around the city. We were determined that even if we had to search the remotest sections of the city, we would locate and acquire the finest shells of the Japanese seas, renowned for their beauty.

We traveled through a noisy, restless, pushing, overcrowded metropolis that is possibly even more

Western and hectic than Western cities themselves. In the busiest center, however, like a great green-and-black jewel, sits the emperor's palace: green for the beautiful enormous lawns and trees that surround the palace, keeping it out of sight, and black for the impressive, heavy stone wall that descends to and is reflected in a wide moat, thus doubling the grand and peaceful picture. There is a gate in the same grand manner—that is, incredibly large. The taxi driver pointed to the gate and told us, "Here I had the most venerable experience of my life." The word sounded strange in conversation, but there it was. "I was driving an American diplomat and the guard let me proceed through the emperor's gate." This is an honor reserved only for invited diplomats and guests of the emperor, preserving his cherished privacy.

It is known, of course, that the emperor of Japan is the foremost shell collector of the land; this makes shell collecting not only fashionable but also stimulates people of all social levels to competition. We shall never forget visiting the house of a notable collector-scientist in Kyoto whose vast collection, it was whispered, was more complete than the emperor's. (Such statements, naturally, are never made aloud.) The dignity of his home, with its doors wide open to the gardens all around, seemed to make it literally a "museum without walls." We vividly recall the simple austerity of the setting as we knelt or sat on the matted floor around our wise and friendly host, a company of four brought together by a common interest. New and beautiful shells were brought in constantly by the master's disciples, disappearing swiftly after we had admired them to make place for still more beautiful shells. Certain rare shells were delicately lifted from their boxes by our host and placed on a low table before us. When this happened, the conversation of the Japanese ceased and everyone contemplated the piece with intense interest. The atmosphere, beginning in a relaxed mood, had now become ceremonial.

Three hours and thousands of shells later when we took our leave, we felt ourselves enriched and refreshed by an experience of mysterious spiritual strength. Still under the spell of the ritualistic contemplation of the shells, we groped awkwardly for words of thanks, the interpreter making no attempt to translate what we were trying to say. Apparently our host understood perfectly. His indulgent smile seemed to tell us, "Don't thank me, thank the shells." What he said in reality was, "You have not seen half my collection."

From Kyoto we traveled to Hong Kong, which proved to be disappointing as far as shells were concerned, and from Hong Kong we extended our journey to the Philippines, Australia, New Zealand, the Fiji and Solomon Islands, and on to Tahiti and Hawaii. From this one trip we brought home a collection of some fifteen thousand shells.

The festive opening of our first exhibition was a success. There was an atmosphere of gay curiosity and excitement. The show was well attended by friends, artists, and the press, and the initial enthusiasm of this small group made itself felt at once in ever-widening circles. Within eight days, handsome photographs and an article had appeared in the *New York Times*, a piece by Emily Genauer had been published in the *New York Herald-Tribune*, and Aline Saarinen had displayed our shells on NBC television as the theme for one of her original visual essays. For weeks the gallery was besieged by photographers, all of them anxious to exploit the new copy that had been discovered.

The original black-and-white newspaper photographs now turned into elaborate color spreads. A few months after the opening show, the elegant quarterly *Horizon* carried an eight-page selection of our shells; at about the same time, *The News*, New York's largest-circulation paper, ran a full-color page in its Sunday magazine section. It is unfortunately impossible to mention here the names of all the magazines that showed interest in our venture.

Quite naturally, to the scientist and the serious amateur, the "Oh-my-how-pretty" response to the shell leaves much—if not everything—to be desired. We agree with this sentiment wholeheartedly, but our experience has been that if the shell is displayed with proper respect for its dignity and singularity, it can elicit from the viewer something much more than familiar clichés. A Long Island housewife, mother of five, said after a quiet half hour in the gallery, "I'm not religious, but when I look at them I believe in God." An Irish poet mumbled something like, "They are like love—if you could understand it, it would not exist." A smart designer, choosing shells for a Fifth Avenue window display: "Thank you for letting me be in your oasis for a while." Almost everyone asked, "Why don't you write a book?"

"Why don't you write a book?" The idea took root and began to grow. The enthusiasm of the press, architects, designers, and people from all walks of life who came to the gallery gave us reason to believe that we ought to open our doors to an even wider public. This volume is an attempt to do just that: to welcome thousands to a world of enchantment whose joys we have witnessed on the faces of the necessarily limited few who were able to visit the gallery itself.

Knowing our limitations, we have not attempted any kind of systematic classification of shells. We have tried instead to let the shells speak for themselves in their own language, to permit the art of the photographer to help them articulate their own essence. A bibliography at the end of the book will direct interested readers to authoritative texts. From this point, those who wish to continue the journey may select whatever aspect seems to them most attractive and inviting. This book is intended as an introduction to a great world of beauty as yet largely unexplored, an invitation to enter that world and *see*. Although its focus is aesthetically directed, the information herein is scientifically correct. Because of the enthusiasm generated by our modest beginning, we believe that there is a corresponding reservoir of enthusiasm that can be reached only through the medium of the book.

SHELLS AND MAN

From the beginning of time, the shell and its animal builder have played an important role in the life of man. Fossil shells of the Paleozoic era have been found throughout the world, the famous Nautiloidea being among the most spectacular, measuring at times up to eight feet in diameter. (The largest shells found today are the giant clams, *Tridacna gigas*, of the western Pacific—up to four feet in length.) The large fossil Nautili are believed to be about 360,000,000 years old, and when we consider that life under water is at times much more difficult to trace than life on land, we can only imagine the myriad evolutions that took place over these eons, change after infinitesimal change, finally leading to our present complex world of sea life. The huge amount of material gathered about this particular branch of life under water makes up the body of the science—malacology.

Malacology defines the life of the animal itself, centering on its biological functions and including its shell-building activities; conchology, in its original usage, focused on the shell and merely speculated—owing to lack of information—on its inner life. The term "conchology" today has a nostalgic flavor, honoring the great scientists of the seventeenth, eighteenth, and nineteenth centuries for whom the term was all-inclusive. Today, malacology is the all-inclusive science, and conchology has become a special branch of study for the amateur scientist and collector. Therefore, the biological history of the mollusk per se will not be the goal of our investigations here. This comparatively new science embraces a field so vast that it has to be divided in sections and each section expounded by specialized scientists. What we wish to do is to explore the extraordinarily complicated relationship between man and shell.

Like a thread of vivid color woven into the tapestry of man's existence, the shell leads us through its own singular history. Its presence is brightly felt throughout mythology, leading us into the dimness of prehistory. Over an immense period of time, the story of the shell in relation to man emerges as a wondrous tale and one of multiple meaning.

The first part of the story, very much in evidence and well known, concerns the practical use of the shell for tools, decorations, and jewelry in primitive civilizations. As the story unfolds, simple practicality gives way to sophistication—ultrasophistication in some cases. The purple of the Tyrians, for example, was a complicated economic factor in the Mediterranean area for many hundreds of years, and the use of mother-of-pearl over thousands of years has only recently diminished, giving way to competitive plastic imitations. Another still growing industry, and very successful today, is that of the Japanese cultured pearl.

SHELLS AS AN ECONOMIC FACTOR

Man's attachment to shells throughout history was conceived under manifold influences. The aesthetic and spiritual relationship interests us especially, because of its reflection in the arts. The shell tribute that the ancient Aztecs paid to the Emperor Montezuma was far from being the only instance of the shell being used as money. It has been so used in many countries and at different times and for different purposes. One use was as a strictly commercial currency of an established standard to enable its owner to buy needed objects. Among the uses of Money Cowries (as the small oval off-white shells arranged in strings were called) was as a decoration for the bodies of African dancers, who with this magic power won special favors from the spirit world. The *Cypraea moneta* (plate 41, right) seems to have been a favorite of many African tribes, serving both functions (figure 1). We have seen contemporary Sudanese natives, beautifully formed young men with ornamental chains of cowries all over their bodies, engaged in a ritual dance imploring the spirits to grant rain for their crops. Also familiar is the beguiling female dancer who tries to attract the man she loves with her cowries tightened around her hair, forehead, and hips to enhance the charm of her sensual dance. The same Money Cowries, in strands or loose in bags, have been used strictly for buying and selling, from village marketing to transactions on a large scale, particularly by Arab traders and the tribes of West Africa throughout the Bight of Benin to Timbuktu and around Lake Chad. Well known among varieties of so-called native money are the strings of shell disks called *sapisapi* in New Guinea and *diwara* and *rongo* in the Melanesian islands, and the wampum of the North American Indians of the East Coast.

Wampum also consisted of strings of shells, but the resemblance with Money Cowries ended there. Instead of single shells pierced and strung together, the American Indians cut cylindrical shapes out of a different shell, a bivalve. The less precious strings were white; the more valuable ones were made of the purple part of various clam shells. One of the earliest references to an established equivalent between Indian wampum and "white-man's coinage" in Virginia in the years 1606 to 1612 gives "a cubit's length valuing six pence." Wampum continued to be used as money through the first half of the eighteenth century. After that time, due mostly to counterfeiting by substituting cheaper material or adding artificial coloring to make it resemble more valuable beads and even using forms of mass production, wampum was no longer employed as currency. Through the nineteenth century, however, for the purpose of gift exchange between Indian tribes or between Indians and whites, wampum, mostly in the form of ceremonial belts, was of great importance, and the belts have historical value today.

A great deal of work was involved in the manufacturing of these strands of shell money, and their worth depended on the rarity of the shells. Some of these primitive shell currencies have even served in recent times to make small change for European money. The image of the cowrie as a type of currency was so strong that the first oval metal coin minted in the Greek colony of Lydia around 670 B.C. was modeled after that shell.

Figure 1. Dancers. Gold Coast, Africa

Many primitive peoples today still employ the shell in their rites and dances. These Africans have wrapped their bodies in strands of small cowries. The shells possibly have a magical function or a sexual symbolism in addition to being used for adornment.

Figure 2. PETER PAUL RUBENS. *Maria de' Medici Landing in Marseilles* (detail). 1625. Oil on canvas. The Louvre, Paris

Throughout the ages and in most parts of the world, triton shells have been employed as musical instruments. Because of this it was only natural that artists should depict mythological sea creatures blowing fanfares on shells modeled after the *Charonia tritonis*. The shell takes its name from the Tritons, who were believed to be the attendants of the sea-god, Neptune.

Figure 3. House of Shells (*Casa de las Conchas*),
Salamanca, Spain. Early 16th century

The austere shape of this Spanish house is relieved by the delicate
carvings around the windows, the magnificent decoration over its
front door, and by the myriad stone scallop shells set into the walls
at regular intervals. The reason for this unusual decoration, which
appears to be unique, is unknown; possibly it fulfilled a vow to
St. James, or it might have signified some special pilgrimage.

Figure 4. SANDRO BOTTICELLI. *The Calumny of Apelles* (detail)
c. 1495. Uffizi Gallery, Florence

Here are beautifully conceived and painted shell-shaped niches, popular architectural
details in late Roman times, which were revived in Renaissance architecture. The
use of a scallop motif for this purpose was due probably to both the aesthetically
pleasing form and the structural strength of the ribbing.

As early as the fifteenth century B.C., a species of murex became historically important when the people of Tyre and Sidon found a way to extract a purple dye from the mollusk that was to color the robes of the Roman and Byzantine emperors and for hundreds of years impress the minds of people with the richness of its hues (although known as "purple" classically, it actually produced a reddish tint). The Roman consuls and senators wore their togas bordered with this precious color in order to be visible in public above all others. Plutarch mentions that the Greeks found purple cloth in the royal treasury of Persia, its beauty undimmed after two hundred years. The prices of these purple materials were always exceedingly high, and the cloth ranged from wool and silk to linen, the shades from magenta to scarlet or the color of blood. The shell that helped the Tyrians achieve this unusual and coveted effect of color was called *Murex purpura*, and the process through which the dye was made, was a long-kept secret. According to Pliny, the recipe consisted of boiling both the crushed shell and the animal in large caldrons, slowly purifying the liquid and testing its color and quality until a satisfactory result was attained. The purple-dyed cloth was so much in demand and its rarity so celebrated that the immense price it commanded did not diminish its popularity throughout the ancient world.

A RELIGIOUS SYMBOL

Other facets of the shell story take us into lesser known areas and far more complex conceptions. One thread, reaching back to prehistoric times, leads us to the knowledge that the shell played a central role in man's earliest religious experiences, and that its powerful symbolism (basically sexual, for it was first and foremost a female symbol) was renewed in the religions of the great civilizations that followed. Another thread, one of the greatest interest to us, reveals its manifold influence on man's artistic efforts and creative ingenuity throughout the world and at all times. During some eras, the shell seems to be closely joined to mythological and religious symbolism; during others it frees itself completely from religion, man becoming interested in the shell as an inspiring archetype upon which to base aesthetic principles. The small animal's achievement in building with intricate beauty and unending variety, instinctively embodying complex mathematical formulas to create a functional, incredible architecture, must have been the main reason for its persistent importance to the mind of man. The shells found in the most ancient tombs were apparently placed there to give comfort to the dead after all resources of human help had failed. Unadorned or undecorated, their function must have been purely symbolic. We know that in Greek mythology the sea and the shell gave miraculous birth to Aphrodite, goddess of love and beauty; even more ancient cultures had similar beliefs. The presence of the shell in prehistoric graves indicates that its symbolic power was thought to continue beyond life. In the same ancestral burying places, excavations also revealed shell-shaped objects such as jewelry and containers for ointments and cosmetics, the shell being reproduced in metal, wood, stone, and other materials. We cannot find a clear line between the shell as a symbol and as a form magically stimulating man's creative mind.

Up until the present, one shell family with just a few species, the chank (Xancidae or Turbinellidae—plate 107), especially the one native to the Indian Ocean, has been a highly treasured object in Hindu temples. In representations of Vishnu, it is held in one of the hands of the four-armed god, who was regarded as the preserver of continuity (and opposed to Shiva, the god of destruction). There are two differing interpretations of the function of the shell in Vishnu's hand: in one, the god could have used it as a weapon; in the other, as a musical instrument to signal his victory over his opponents.

The so-called left-handed chank plays an even more important role in the hands of the Hindu priest. To explain the word "left-handed" we should know that almost all univalves (shells that consist of one section only, as opposed to the two-part bivalves) rise in a spiral right-handed clockwise movement. There are very few exceptions to this rule, one of them being a left-handed species, *Busycon contrarium* (left-handed whelk), whose whorl turns counterclockwise (plate 92, top).

The left-handed chank mentioned above is an example of a phenomenon for which there is no scientific explanation, the shell of a normally right-handed species building contrary to nature's established functions. These left-handed shells preserve to the minutest details everything necessary to the animal's well-being, and are in every way the exact mirror image of the normal shell. They are of great rarity and therefore very valuable. It may well be that the Hindu priest serving medicine in the holy shell (the left-handed chank, usually decorated with gold and precious stones) to an ailing member of his community has found the strength of belief that gives him the power to produce a miracle. Seeing the shell's perfection in spite of its contrary conception, he is reminded of all the other wonders of creation and its greatness, and this mystical encouragement tends to give success to his performance.

Certain shells have been used as musical instruments for thousands of years in many countries and in many ways: to call believers to prayer, to sound warning in time of danger, to summon warriors for the fight, to ring out triumphantly, marking the entrance of kings and heroes. Neptune's companions, raising their triton shells to welcome Maria de' Medici on her arrival at the coast of France, are an important feature of the foreground of a painting by Rubens, giving his version of this most romantic landing in the harbor of Marseilles (figure 2). The Shinto priests in Japan today use an instrument made of the same large shell (*Charonia tritonis*—plate 50, left, and right top), which has been cut off at the top, the resulting round opening fitted with a small metal mouthpiece. This instrument produces an unbelievably eerie sound when blown to call the faithful to service.

PRE-COLUMBIAN AMERICA

Although sources of proven and authentic fact are scarce, and although evidence of pre-Columbian contacts between the New and Old Worlds has never been satisfactorily established, the more that is learned from excavations and archaeological research in both North and South America, the more we see striking similarities between the great Indian civilizations of the Americas and the great European civilizations of the past.

The symbolic shell is found in some of the earliest archaeological sites in South America—graves in Chile dating around 3000 B.C. We cannot, of course, state with certainty that the concept and symbolism of the Aphrodite of the Greeks parallels those of Peruvian or Toltec fertility goddesses, but we would be inclined to favor this theory. Vases painted with a goddess emerging from a shell, and earthenware sculpture portraying similar themes, lead us to believe that the shells found in the graves of pre-Columbian high priests serving these goddesses are related symbolically to those found in places sacred to the worship of Aphrodite. As there has been no concrete proof of this similarity up to this date, the parallel must remain a theory.

The best-studied pre-Columbian civilizations are chiefly those of Mexico and Central America. Because of the relatively untouched cities found there (the Inca cities were mainly destroyed by the Spaniards), the area has been the subject of intense and methodical archaeological research.

Perhaps the highest civilization of Central America was that of the Mayans, which reached its peak between 300 and 900 A.D. The Mayans have been compared to the Greeks and the Egyptians because of their advanced and sophisticated mathematics and astronomy, and because of their highly developed art and architecture. Mayan mathematical symbols are far simpler in concept than, say, Roman ones, and the Mayans mastered the concept of zero. And the zero is represented in their glyphs by a univalve that appears to be a type of cowrie.

The culture hero of the Mayans (and of the Toltecs and Aztecs) was a god named variously Quetzalcoatl or Kulkulkan. This deity unites in his personality and powers many facets that seem familiar to us. Like the Hindu Vishnu, he is the patron god of creativity in art, science, and agriculture, and is opposed to the gods of destruction, who constantly seek to undermine his power.

Quetzalcoatl's beginnings or nativity are the subject of various legends among the Mesoamerican Indians; one of the more popular depicts his emergence, full-grown, from the shell of a gastropod. One of the many temples dedicated to him, in Teotihuacan, is decorated with alternating univalves and bivalves—the two great divisions of the shell world. Quetzalcoatl was also supposed to have lived in a palace built of shells. Like the one mentioned above, most of his temples are richly decorated with shells, and the god is often shown seated on a pedestal carved in the form of a shell.

The exact symbolism of Quetzalcoatl's shells is still to be decided. Was the shell a sexual symbol, a symbol of regeneration, or a symbol of death or vanity (the shell without the creature it houses is empty of life, like a skull)? So far, we do not know. But we do know that shells played a large part in the religion and life of the pre-Columbian Indians.

In contrast to the great past civilizations of the Old World, the "classic period" of the New World is still relatively unknown to us (one of the reasons being that most of its writings were destroyed by the Spaniards, and those that have survived have not yet been completely deciphered). However, one document dating from the time of the Conquest has shed considerable light on Aztec civilization. In 1521, many Aztec records were included in a report to the first Spanish viceroy, Don Antonio Mendoza. This manuscript, known as the Codex Mendoza, is now in the Bodleian Library at Oxford. It includes lists of gifts rendered by various tribes to Montezuma. Among the treasures named are eight hundred shells. These were probably the red *Spondylus americanus*, which is native to Mexican coastal waters (plates 159, 160). Although relatively common, they must have had a special value for the Aztecs, although we do not yet know why they were such desirable objects that they were included in the emperor's tribute.

They were much used by the Aztecs and Mayans; they were a featured cult symbol at burial ceremonies for important Mayan personalities, and were also used as the red portions in the precious turquoise inlay-work of the Mayans and Aztecs.

A highly stylized representation of the *Spondylus americanus* also serves as a name-glyph in the Codex Mendoza. It represents the equivalent of several letters of our alphabet and is used in the formation of one syllable of a three-syllable word standing for the name of a town.

The pre-Columbian civilizations also employed shells as containers for perfumes or ointments, using either the shell itself or its representation carried out in gold, silver, or even pottery. As we stated above, the shell's symbolic value is still unknown, but Mayan graves have been excavated in which are found three kinds of shells that have been used as receptacles for the most precious symbolic objects of the Mayan religion: jade and cinnabar. They were apparently placed there to accompany the soul beyond the grave and to act as a solace and a talisman on its journey to the underworld. The shells that have been most used for these ritualistic purposes are the *Spondylus americanus*, the equally beautiful *Lyropecten nodosus* (plates 155, 156), and a scallop resembling the *Pecten jacobaeus*.

Contrary to the civilizations of the Old World, the early Americans also included in their symbolic rites the shells of gastropods. Found in very early graves, these may have had a connection with the cult of Quetzalcoatl, who as we have seen was born from a gastropod shell.

When we look at pre-Columbian sculpture, we do not need any ethnological information about the way of life of the people of that period: the sculpture speaks an eloquent language of its own. Unfortunately, it is often referred to as "primitive" art; it can only be so termed in relation to works of Hellenistic origin. Our own time has seen a return to an abstraction of natural forms, and since pre-Columbian art displays this tendency, it is currently appreciated and found to be inspiring and close to the expressiveness of modern art. The sculpture possesses great passion, strength, and organization; it is the work of a great culture.

On much pre-Columbian sculpture one may see various representations of the shell, either as a symbol or employed in the inscribed glyphs. Shells themselves were also sculpted out of stone, precious metals, or clay, and these were used as containers or as religious vessels or offerings.

Figure 5. SANDRO BOTTICELLI. *The Birth of Venus* (detail)
c. 1480. Uffizi Gallery, Florence

This is perhaps the most famous depiction of a scallop shell in the world. Botticelli probably used a *Pecten jacobaeus* as a model, but he distorted it somewhat for the sake of composition and movement. Even though not true to nature, it embodies the essence of all scallop shells, and thus may be considered an ideal representation.

Figures 6 and 7. GEORGE MOND (attr.)
Nautilus Cup. 17th century
Nautilus shell, silver, gold, and amethyst, height 13″
Wadsworth Atheneum, Hartford

During the Age of Discovery, European collectors cherished objects that are of little or no rarity today. For instance, coconut shells were mounted in precious metals and used as chalices, ostrich eggs were likewise embellished, and unusual or exotic shells were also made into precious objects. In this German cup, a nautilus shell has been stripped of its periostracum to reveal its lustrous mother-of-pearl surface. This has been engraved with scenes suggesting far-off lands (note the elephant). The lip of the shell has been rimmed in silver-gilt, and the top bears a finial representing a winged toadlike monster. The base is formed by a gold Triton blowing a triton shell. The Triton rides on a tortoise which rests on an amethyst crystal. This in turn is set on a base supported by four cephalopods.

Figure 8. JACOPO DEL ZUCCHI (1542–c. 1590)
The Treasures of the Sea
Oil on canvas, 20⅞ x 17¾″
Borghese Gallery, Rome

In this work the artist seems to be following an old Italian tradition that can be traced back to Roman painting. However, though the general theme and the position of the figures may suggest the Antique, the tone of this picture is typical of the High Renaissance. The four continents seem to be personified here, and beneath their feet lie the treasures brought from the seven seas. This is a work that could only come from the Age of Discovery. The shells shown are mainly idealizations of the real thing, but they sparkle and glisten with a life of their own. Among the shells, one may recognize the artist's version of murices, giant clams, scallops, and turban shells.

THE MIDDLE AGES—
ST. JAMES AND THE SCALLOP SHELL

Christianity had an early and important connection with a certain shell, the scallop. One of the apostles of Christ, James the son of Zebedee, who was a fisherman, was given this shell as an attribute by the early Christians (this shell species eventually became known as *Pecten jacobaeus*, after the saint). The story of this saint, whose image is always adorned in one or another way with the emblem of the symbolic shell, stimulated the arts in various fields. So great was the impact of the story on the imaginations of artists that its influence was felt all over Europe. As a result, we enjoy countless sculptures, paintings, drawings, and illuminated documents reflecting the long years of veneration for St. James, known as Santiago in Spain, the land where he finally rested. Compostela, where the saint was buried after a life of legendary tribulation, had become by the early Middle Ages a desirable goal of travelers seeking spiritual comfort. Pilgrimages restoring the sinner to the state of grace were an important part of religious life. One of the reasons for the attraction that made the small Spanish town one huge center for pilgrims from all over the European world was the fact that it was less perilous and less costly to reach than Jerusalem.

Great attention and affection was given St. James both by pilgrims and artists. We can find a lovely Baroque Madonna in Pontevedra, Spain, clad in robes of embroidered silk and velvet, her beautiful austere head, carved in wood, serenely held above all the frills; her hat is identical to the one worn by St. James himself, with the shell in the center of the turned-up brim. Belonging to a much earlier period, about 1500, this saint and his famous hat can be seen in Kalk, Germany, represented in pure Gothic style in carved and painted wood. Both superb pieces are typical of their times, when the little shell was so well known as the pilgrim's emblem. In Spanish, French, Italian, and English churches, museums, and secular architecture in general, we find countless masterpieces showing the same motif.

As more and more penitents arrived in Compostela, the shell was brought inland from the shore of the Atlantic to be sold in booths near the cathedral, and was usually fastened on the shoulder of the pilgrim's cloak. The image of the shell did more than gain the respect of everyone who saw it, as proof of the wearer's voyage to the holy place. The *Liber Sancti Jacobi*, at Santiago de Compostela, mentions that a knight of Ampulia had been cured of goiter by touching a shell brought home by a pilgrim. Evidently the shell had again reached the importance of a symbol that had the power to regenerate life.

HERALDRY

From its earliest beginnings in the twelfth or thirteenth century, the "minor art" of heraldry made great use of the shell. The coat of arms was reserved at that time, and still is today, as a mark of the socially prominent. The structure of social standings, however, having changed so completely since then, only a shadow of its former importance remains with us.

At their beginning, the heraldic signs were an indispensable badge of recognition in encounters between feuding factions. Besides this practical aspect, the pride of families and their followers was identified with their ingenious and unique coats of arms. At that time, Europe was divided into small units, ruled by innumerable kings, dukes, counts, and barons. These powerful families depended on their knights to fight for them and their interests, to help them organize the territories they owned, and to acquire new lands. It was of the utmost importance to perceive from afar whether friend or foe stood on the field of battle, and the bright colors of heraldry helped do that. With so many small communities involved, conflicts of interest arose constantly everywhere, and the prowess and pageantry of the time made the coat of arms a great artistic success and indispensable in a practical sense to the ruling classes.

One of the important forms of heraldry today, the flag, still inspires our deep-rooted loyalties, but there cannot be any comparison with the absolute necessity of armory (another name for heraldry) at a time when communication was primitive.

The Most Noble Order of the Garter was founded in England in the middle of the fourteenth century, and since then more than seven hundred members have been received into it. The granting of this distinguished honor included the designing of a new coat of arms, very often adorned with scallops and other shells. Two great English aristocrats in our time who were made Knights of the Garter, Sir Winston Churchill and Sir Anthony Eden, have scallops on their armorial bearings. Once more the scallop gave its decorative image to art—even though a "minor" art—and demonstrated its perennial popularity.

THE RENAISSANCE

The Renaissance, as we know, brought forth great ideas developed by prolific personalities of immense talent. The closeness and devotion that the Middle Ages had felt for the Church underwent many changes, and almost everything built in the new style was rich and decorative. Piety and simplicity began to disappear; the lofty emotional atmosphere that the Gothic style conveyed now gave way to elegance and worldliness, whether in churches, palaces, or fountains. Yet in spite of the birth of new ideas, with completely new values affecting habits, thinking, and worship in all parts of Europe, the shell again found a place of prominence. No longer the symbol of saints or the magic receptacle for a priest's healing potion, it was admired and cherished as an example of superior architectural mastery.

Leonardo da Vinci, whose genius is timeless, recognized the beauty and functional perfection of the shell's spiral structure. He studied nature's capable builders thoroughly and made drawings utilizing the inventive construction of a certain univalve mollusk as the inspiration for the design of a spiral staircase. This drawing still exists, and is supposed to have been the model for the exquisite and historically famous staircase of the Château of Blois in France.

More and more the virtuoso artist lost interest in the depth of religious feeling and saw the saint or Madonna only as a pretext for painting works of rich color, elaborate composition, and triumphant technical innovation. The same formality obtained in sculpture and architecture. The scallop shell was again used for decorative effect in fountains or for water basins of cool marble carved in its shape. The scallop was also employed as a motif applied in relief to the outside of palaces. One of them, the so-called House of Shells in Salamanca, is among the most celebrated, and richly deserves its great fame (figure 3).

In Rome, the impact of the High Renaissance was strongest and has given the city much of its character, which has endured to the present day. At the time of the ancient Romans, shell forms were part of their architecture, and it was only natural that the innate elegance that had proved so successful then would be revived in the new era. A listing of great churches, sculptures, altars, porticoes, and tapestries with the shell as motif or as model of construction would be endless, and the names of their creators among the most famous. For instance, Bramante's Tempietto in Rome, which was the forerunner of St. Peter's, is decorated inside and out with scallop-shaped niches.

The Renaissance is of particular interest to our survey because it granted such a multitude of uses to the preferred shell form of the era, the scallop. Architects had so frequently borrowed its image for niches, façades, tombs, and pedestals that all other artists had to follow suit.

Verrocchio used the shell on many occasions; in the Cathedral of Pistoia we find his painting (c. 1480) depicting the Madonna and Child seated under a shell-shaped canopy. A sculpture by the same artist, *The Doubting Thomas with Christ* (c. 1465) made for a tabernacle created by Donatello, stands in a shell-shaped niche in the church of Or San Michele in Florence. Correggio used them in his frescoes at Parma. In the cupola of the cathedral, four saints are represented in large frescoes using highly stylized large and small shells (1526–30). Also in Parma, for the pendentives below the dome of the Convent of San Paolo, Correggio created groups of figures, each surrounded by shells. Botticelli was greatly interested in the different aspects of the indispensable shell motif. In *The Calumny of Apelles*, he set his protagonists in an architectural setting based on ancient Roman models, with sculptures standing in niches formed like shells (figure 4). Another of his exploitations of the scallop motif may be seen in an Annunciation, where he uses it as a portico, in the center of which he places a coat of arms. And his lovely *Birth of Venus* (figure 5), painted in the spirit of the mystical Greek legend even if the attendant figures surrounding the goddess wear Renaissance robes, displays one of the most famous depictions of a scallop shell.

THE LATE RENAISSANCE AND
THE BAROQUE

During the Late Renaissance, many gold- and silversmiths created magnificent pieces from heraldic motifs; this type of work flourished up through the Baroque period, and many superb examples of the craft exist. Shells were used in extravagantly lavish pieces, often coming from the workshops of the most famous artists, Benvenuto Cellini among the foremost. The shell was sometimes displayed in its natural form as a cup placed on or surrounded by figures of cast or wrought gold. At other times it was used for elaborate goblets and dishes, and brought splendor to the tables of kings. This ornateness was also reflected in vessels for the Church.

Some very well-known pieces can be seen in New York's Metropolitan Museum of Art, and other similar ones are shown in many museums and collections throughout the world. An outstanding work in this genre is a mounted nautilus dating from the first half of the sixteenth century, which can be seen in the Lazaro Galdiano Museum in Madrid. The shell is shown in its natural colors—white with reddish-brown stripes—the black "beak" stripped down to reveal the lustrous mother-of-pearl beneath. In this state, the shell is ornamented with a rich gold rim around the lip, a base sculptured like a turtle, and on top of the arrangement a mythical animal ridden by a *putto* (a cherubic infant), triton in hand. Though perhaps excessively decorated, it is so masterful in execution that one can see why variations on the theme were popular (figures 6, 7).

The European scene was undergoing violent change. Courageous and adventurous men had set forth on the seas and were returning with trophies and undreamed-of riches. Columbus had landed in the Americas at the end of the fifteenth century, and others quickly followed. Europe was vibrant with excitement over every object brought from the New World, and people were avidly trying to surround themselves with exotica arriving from that strange land (figure 8). The shell at once took a very important place among the new treasures, and soon fascinated the wealthy to the extent that they started to collect the amazing variety of these sensitive animals' complicated buildings (figure 9). It was the beginning of a new serious interest in the shell and the creature that lived in it. People wanted more knowledge about the living animal's habits and its fantastic architectural capabilities. As time went on, attempts at organized thinking and collecting were made, a beginning from which slowly emerged a new science, conchology, the natural history of sea shells. The process was painful. The collector was rather romantically involved with his acquisitions, and his goals were those of a rich man counting his treasures and proudly displaying them in elaborate cabinetry (figure 10).

The new infatuation with shells reached its highest peak in Amsterdam, the Dutch being one of the first to bring rare cargoes home from the little-known continents. Dutch artists re-revived interest in

Figure 9. EMMANUEL(?) DE CRITZ
John Tradescant and Zythepsa. c. 1645
Oil on canvas. Ashmolean Museum, Oxford

The elder and younger John Tradescant were English naturalists and explorers. The elder amassed a great collection of shells, which was the finest extant at that time. This was inherited by his son, who is shown here with a Quaker friend (whose unusual name was an adopted one) and a portion of the famous shell collection. Among the specimens shown are a *Conus marmoreus* at bottom left, a turban at its right, and next to it a superb triton.

Figure 10. F. H. FRANCKEN THE YOUNGER
Cabinet d'Amateur. 1619. Oil on panel, 22½ x 33½″
Musée Royal des Beaux Arts, Antwerp

This painting typifies the collecting mania which swept through Europe (especially the Low Countries) in the sixteenth and seventeenth centuries. The collection shown here contains a little bit of everything: coins and medallions, stones, Antique glass, letters or documents, jewelry, flowers (representing the tulipomania of the time?), paintings and drawings, specimens of marine life (note the dried seahorse), and, of course, shells. Although the majority of these collections were based upon the exotic aspects of the objects, the quality of the items was usually excellent, and, as seen here, was combined with a considerable amount of good taste.

Figure 11. BALTHASAR VAN DER AST
(c. 1590–c. 1656). *Still Life with Shells*
Oil on canvas, 11¾ x 18½"
Boymans–van Beuningen Museum, Rotterdam

The Dutch predilection for still lifes was admirably suited to shells. The people of the time were avid collectors of shells (both for their exotic appearance and simply because they were rare, and therefore eminently collectable); the realistic rendering of shells provided a pleasant game in which the artist could exercise his skill. This exquisite composition contains miter shells, a turban and a turrid shell, several cones and murices, a cowrie, and others, which contrast superbly with the cherries and currants, and also with the insects flying above them.

Figure 12. REMBRANDT. *The Shell*. 1650
Etching. Rijksmuseum, Amsterdam

Rembrandt's depiction of a *Conus marmoreus* is not only a magnificent etching; it is also a correct delineation of this shell—except for one point: Rembrandt neglected to reverse his drawing on the metal plate, so that when printed the shell appears to be a left-handed specimen, and therefore a great rarity. Note, however, that Rembrandt carefully etched his name on the plate in reverse, so that his signature is not a mirror image.

the shell, and it is duly included in their compositions (figure 11). Among other works, a lovely Rembrandt etching of *Conus marmoreus* (Marble Cone) dated 1650 stands out (figure 12). The simplicity and soberness of the great master's approach to the shell is in complete contrast to the Baroque and to the playful renditions of accumulated garlands of the still lifes other artists created.

THE EIGHTEENTH CENTURY—ROCOCO

At the courts of European kings in the eighteenth century, especially the French court under the reigns of the luxury-loving monarchs Louis XIV and Louis XV, decoration reached a peak of resplendency. Palaces, mansions, churches, and gardens were tricked out in a style whose aim was toward looseness of composition, extravagance of form, and a fantastic disregard for what we now consider "good taste." Walls, ceilings, paintings, sculptures, furniture, and landscaping all displayed surfaces that exploded into colorful, light-catching facets.

The term "Rococo" derives from the French "*rocaille,*" a type of rock-and-shell decoration employed in the construction of grottoes and pleasances. "*Rocaille,*" in turn, derives from the expression "*travail de coquille,*" which means "shell work." The relation between shell forms and the basic forms of the Rococo style are perhaps best exemplified in the shapes and colors of the specimens shown in plates 57–80. These shells are ideal examples, and one could almost believe that many could have been created by the great porcelainists of the Rococo.

At its height, this style quickly degenerated into pure frivolity. Despite this, however, its influence spread throughout Continental Europe, although its choicest flowering was mainly in France, Germany, and Austria. Even the simplest objects of everyday life—tableware, accessories, even boxes of all kinds—were shaped like shells or erupted with shell forms of the wildest kind. The austere and symbolic past of the shell form was buried and forgotten under an avalanche of exuberance. The grandiose simplicity of Greek and Roman architectural ornament and the dignified formality of the Renaissance use of shell forms was obscured. All that mattered now was the decoration of the surface. In Christian symbolism the shell signified purity, resurrection, redemption on the Day of Judgment, and forgiveness through pilgrimage. The Rococo laughingly discarded any touch of such religious sentiment, and treated the shell as a joyous design element, a charming, fanciful, lively object whose aesthetic appearance embodied a whole repertory of forms and colors that served to inspire gilded and polychrome ornaments for interior decoration.

THE VICTORIAN APPROACH

The sentimental decor of the Victorian period has still a great hold on us, perhaps because there is so little space left for sentiment in our present hectic activities and our great responsibilities. The first hint of the vulgarization of the long respected and admired shell can be detected at that time, continuing to the middle of the twentieth century, when it reached its lowest point. Nevertheless, there were moments of beauty. Royalty and aristocrats on occasion surrounded themselves with charming fantasies made of shells. Prior to the Victorian era, so-called follies—grottoes, pavilions, and fountains all gay and luxurious—could be found in England, France, Italy, and even Germany.

One of the most gracious of these, and the most often reproduced, is the scintillating shell pavilion at Goodwood Park, Sussex, dating from the middle of the eighteenth century. Two shell figurines of a later period already reflect typical Victorian taste: the handling of the shells is skillful but not inspired, very charming but with an inclination toward saccharine sweetness.

The Victorian interior cluttered with trinkets must have been enjoyed by the rich and the middle classes. The trophies and carpets brought from the Orient, the ivory-inlaid screens, the heavy velvet curtains—all conspired to create an atmosphere of romance. The shell was used in the same spirit. We have followed it through the history of religious symbolism in ancient Greece and Rome to the Christianity of the Middle Ages, and have seen its use in the religious rituals of the Indians of pre-Columbian America, and the supernatural powers attributed to it by African tribes and many other civilizations. All this ended in the nineteenth century. The shell had lost its stature and was no longer a tool of creation; but it remained in the hearts of the people of the Victorian era as a messenger from the shores of faraway places, bringing with it the atmosphere of extraordinary, exciting voyages. It also served in decorations of a romantic nature. Stuffed under a glass bell in an abundance of shapes and colors, shells made quaint pictures very much in the spirit of Victorian taste.

Another typical object of the time was the "sailor's valentine." This was a touching souvenir sent home by sailors from their expeditions overseas, consisting of a wooden box, the two halves united by a hinge, revealing when opened an awkward but thereby more endearing composition made of shells. Sometimes a few words were added: "Remember Me" or "The Giver Loves You."

Victorian decor had a great affinity for the shell, even greater than that of former periods; a complicated arrangement, or one or two shells alone, was a must on every mantelpiece. Sometimes a spotted cowrie engraved with the donor's name made its appearance, sometimes a mother-of-pearl turban shell. This unfortunate manner of display certainly contributed to the total downfall of a world of admiration that had accompanied the shell through the centuries. Its spiritual value as a symbol in ancient times had been long lost, and finally even its romantic quality sadly disappeared, along with the stuffy, enclosed style of the Victorian era, unendurable to the new generation.

We think that in the United States, where our tastes vacillate more vehemently than in other countries, the shell has been perhaps more degraded than anywhere else. The seashore is now open to almost everyone: a trip that earlier was possible only for the very wealthy is now enjoyed by millions. Present trends seem to have begun in England when the Prince Regent built the Brighton Pavilion and his followers made it fashionable to collect shells at the seashore. Later it became popular everywhere, and commercial enterprises were established to accommodate a large field of new customers.

THE EMERGING SCIENCE OF MALACOLOGY

The nautilus (argonaut), an incredibly precise builder, attracted Aristotle's attention on one of his voyages, and he brought back glowing records of his observations. Even if they were not all scientifically correct, his ideas were far ahead of those of his contemporaries, and his conclusions were believed and stood valid for a long time. His incisive mind and the enthusiasm of his description inspired a lovely nineteenth-century engraving in Cassell's *Natural History*, showing the well-shaped nautilus (*Argonauta*) floating gracefully on calm seas. Seated in this romantic-looking vessel, a fantastic creature uses its shapely extremities to give direction and equilibrium to its navigation. Nobody could guess that what we see is an octopus taking care of its duties as a mother. Aristotle saw only the extraordinary beauty of the animal's behavior and the elegance of the shell form in which it was traveling.

Jules Verne's *Twenty Thousand Leagues under the Sea* anticipated the invention of the submarine and was inspired by a similar cephalopod's mathematical exploits. Verne's shell model was the Chambered Nautilus: Captain Nemo's submarine, the "Nautilus," though not shaped like its shell namesake, was separated into many compartments—a typical feature of the nautilus. To appreciate fully these shells' magnificent shape, one has to see what superior organization the growing animal creates inside its house. Every one of its air chambers is arranged in geometrically correct progression beginning with the young animal's diminutive first cell, the chambers becoming larger and larger, always turning precisely in the exact volute of its outer shell (plate 186). From first to last chamber, the octopus-like animal provides for a channel (the siphonal canal) to enable it to reach the innermost chambers, helping it move with more ease at great depths on the bottom of the ocean. The creature observed by Aristotle is the so-called Paper Nautilus, or as Linnaeus later named it, the argonaut (plate 187), whose paper-thin walls turn in the same graceful outer volute as its cousin's, the Chambered Nautilus. Aristotle's "nautilus" is not a shell but an egg case that the female of this species builds from her secretions to house and protect her eggs until they hatch. This egg case retains its great beauty after it has served its purpose, and is a popular example of the molluscan world's building ability.

Even though Carolus Linnaeus, the famous Swedish naturalist, lived in the middle of the eighteenth century, the breakthrough in scientific collecting came only in the nineteenth century. Important scientists began publishing illustrated books—beginning with Swainson's *Exotic Conchology* in 1821 and Reeve's *Conchologia Iconica* in 1843, which are outstanding examples in this field. The illustrations aimed at the exactness and sophistication of the miniature paintings of contemporaneous artists and are so exquisitely executed that they remain unsurpassed to this day. In the newly found underwater world there was so much information to be classified, some of it ill-defined, that scientists did not try to give new names to each new specimen. In many cases colloquial terms were retained, translated literally into Latin. Thus Fly Dirt, so called by sailors because of its flyspecked markings, became, in scientific nomenclature, *Conus stercusmuscarum* (plate 136, number 7). This accounts for a certain oddness here and there in Latin terms.

The European advance of systematic studies of the shell continued steadily from the beginning of the eighteenth century on. We can mention only a few of the many famous scientists who contributed to conchological research of this time, and one of the most astute certainly was Rumphius. Since he was in the service of the Dutch East India Company, his extensive travels enabled him to observe closely a great amount of material and to make precise notes and comments on the specimens he found. In modern conchology this is the only accepted method, and it was gradually improved through new diving techniques and especially through dredging.

Charles W. Thomson was the first scientist to realize the importance of biological conditions in the deep sea. He learned of dredging experiments undertaken on the coast of Norway by Michael Sars, and in 1868 and 1869, when he obtained from the British government the loan of two ships, he made two successive trips using this new method himself. Later he described his findings in a book called *The Depths of the Sea*. His studies proved that animal life exists in abundance to the depth of 650 fathoms, and also made clear several other conditions of great significance for the development of life under water. In 1872 he was given the "H.M.S. Challenger" for his most important trip, a circumnavigation of the globe, and cruised as the head of a staff of scientists for three and a half years, earning great honors on his return. From 1831 to 1836, Darwin had made his famous voyage on the "Beagle," publishing his revolutionary theories with the help of material he had collected during the years of his surveying expeditions.

THE SHELL IN THE TWENTIETH CENTURY

Objects manufactured of shells reached great popularity in the early nineteen-hundreds. A catalogue of a Brighton shell merchant of that time lists an astonishing number of articles made of, or decorated with, shells. These souvenirs, which formerly had a romantic flavor, now became impersonal and commercial.

Figure 13. PIERRE PUGET
Atlas from the portal of the Town Hall,
Toulon. 1656

Here is an unusual example of shells employed as architectural decoration. As has
been noted in this book, the scallop shell
seems to have been the most popular shell
form used in architecture. Here, however,
other shells have been used. The garland
below the figure's waist is supported by a
type of turban shell, the figure itself terminates in a pair of crossed, stylized triton
shells, and the ornamentation terminates in
a scallop shell.

Figure 14. JAMES ENSOR. *Les Coquillages*, 1895. Oil on canvas, 32½ x 43″
Collection Dr. and Mrs. Howard Sirak, Columbus, Ohio

The Belgian painter Ensor felt a great affinity for the sea and for the life of the sea. His family
ran a number of shops in Ostend, and when Ensor was a child, the shells piled up on shelves
and counters fascinated him. In many of his paintings he employs shells as part of the composition, often grouping them in bizarre combinations with skulls, skeletons, and masks.
In this painting he was content to let the forms and colors of the shells speak for themselves.
Among the specimens included one may recognize a *Charonia tritonis* at right, a *Cassis
tuberosa* top center, and a *Strombus gigas* at left.

Figure 15. ODILON REDON. *The Birth of Venus*. c. 1912
Oil on canvas, 55½ x 24″. Collection Stephen Higgons, Paris

For thousands of years the traditional representations of the birth of Venus had depicted the goddess emerging from the shell of a bivalve, namely a scallop. This painting seems to be the first time that the goddess has been shown issuing from a univalve (which appears to be an idealization of a Queen Conch). Redon, a sensitive artist whose works were imbued with Hermetic mysticism, perhaps delved back into the misty beginnings of all myths, and decided to give his interpretation a double symbolism combining iconographic symbols of love and birth.

Our time has added a few new ideas to the list—"amusing" animals made of shells from Japan, shell jewelry from the Florida coast—but the crucifixes, paperweights, purses, picture frames, and all the other articles of this lively industry were already in production at the turn of the century.

Far be it from us to condemn a phenomenon that brought pleasure to so many: objects, values, and events of greater importance have undergone a similar misuse and misinterpretation in our time. Our formerly revered holidays have become noisy and commercialized; the display of false splendor is discarded in a day. In a completely different field, the shell has suffered the same fate. Wherever we see shells, except in a museum, they are cut, polished, filed, painted, or glued together to make "cute" objects that are not functional, or costume jewelry that any smart woman would reject. There are exceptions, of course, but these only prove that the "gift from the sea," as Anne Morrow Lindbergh so eloquently calls it, is today totally misunderstood.

We are happy to note, however, that the recent progress in the science of malacology has been great. Several museums and universities have their organized staffs of working members headed by a leading scientist. Problems are worked out together or, more often, divided into areas of specialization. In this way the scientists give their attention to the minutest detail in reporting their research and can add to the overall knowledge with new observations of their own. The advancement of science has been as great as the decline in the aesthetic appreciation or admiring affection that the shell formerly commanded. It is not understandable why, despite our meager chances to refresh ourselves, to retire from the wear and tear of daily existence, there is so small a public attraction to the shell and the simplicity of the beauty it offers.

We are not referring to the serious collector; he usually has years of experience and study, and is informed enough to appreciate beautiful specimens or photographic reproductions of them. They may help him enlarge his acquaintance with the subject and check on his favorites. Since we are collectors ourselves and speak to those who come to see our exhibitions, we have heard many memorable remarks reflecting upon the personalities of our visitors and the quality of their interest in shells. We have noticed that some people who have seen shells in elegant shops in Paris have been convinced that buying shells is the thing to do or is "in." Wealthy Americans have brought back from France the handsome *Spondylus americanus* or American Chrysanthemum Shell (plates 159, 160), not realizing that this oyster comes from American waters only and had to be exported to France to attract their attention. If this example is extreme, there are many similar ones.

We welcome every way in which a shell is exposed to the public if it has been found alive, and if it also has been cleaned the right way. Unfortunately, these conditions very rarely exist; this kind of specimen is hard to obtain, and to a certain extent the trading in it is comparable to that in precious stones. Every move to obtain a specimen requires not only a knowledge of the shell but also of the market value, which fluctuates. Depending on the year, the harvest might be very good or very poor, and because of advances in techniques of dredging, values become less predictable every day. All this should not discourage one from collecting seriously or from merely acquiring shells for no other reason than their delightful looks and the integrity of their beauty. Among the least expensive shells are many remarkably beautiful specimens.

The murex recently came to the attention of the public when, in October, 1957, the Shell Transport and Trading Company published, in celebration of its sixtieth anniversary, *The Scallop*. Even though this publication was devoted to the shell that had become the company's trademark, the stylized scallop shell, the background of the whole story involves other shell families and has its beginnings in Victorian times. Marcus Samuel, the founder of the original company, which catered to the needs of ships and sailors, started his business in London in a district frequented by sailors of homecoming ships. As a sideline, he started collecting shells, particularly those from the Far East. These were often mounted in boxes and sold. Eventually, the trade and transport business became so successful under his and his brother's leadership that at the time of his death and the liquidation of his estate, his heirs were able to build the company's first oil tanker. This ship was given the name "Murex" in homage to the elder Samuel and his attachment to shells, and was the first of a fleet of ships all named after different genera. The scallop shell that the company uses now as an emblem belongs, of course, to another family, but was chosen in the same spirit—to honor its shell-loving founder.

The story of the Shell Oil Company brings us to the present, in which few, or at least we think too few, great artists and personalities have any preoccupation with the shell (figures 14, 15). The Spanish artist Joan Miró had shells in mind when he used an actual pecten shell in a collage some years ago, and more recently a cowrie shell was painted by him to represent the head of a woman, with three dots acting as the nose and eyes. This work must have been created in the spirit of the symbolism of old primitive civilizations.

An American artist of our time who gave the shell a tremendous accolade was Frank Lloyd Wright; his touch of genius is still in our midst and part of our daily life. It might be that, living for a long time in Japan, he absorbed much of the Japanese culture, its sensitive and organized approach to building small or large, its admiration for the systematic while still retaining freedom from dogma. All this is exemplified in the shell. Exerting a powerful influence as a teacher, Wright did much to bring closer to his students his own great admiration for the architectural lesson of the shell.

Frank Lloyd Wright sums up his ideas at the end of one of his Taliesin lectures with a statement very much like those we have heard from people looking at shells in our own exhibition rooms:

Here in these shells we see the housing of the life of the sea. It is the housing of a lower order of life, but it is a housing with exactly what we lack—inspired form. In this collection of houses of hundreds of small beings, who themselves built these houses, we see a quality which we call invention. The beauty of their variations is never finished. It is not a question of principle of design. This multitudinous expression indicates what design can mean. Certainly Divinity is here in these shells in their humble form of life.

Formulated in one way or another, the reaction of our visitors continually expresses the need to believe that the creation able to transmit the impact of its greatness with such simplicity cannot fail us.

A friend of ours found a way to express his delight in being introduced to the immense variety of shells and in later discovering for himself the beauty, charm, and wisdom of molluscan shell building. This person combines rare gifts—he is brilliant, witty, and perceptive, and in addition is widely traveled and holds a scholarly position of great importance. When he began to assemble his now impressive collection, he told us: "With these shells a whole new world has opened to me."

Through this book many more may come closer to similar reflections. The beautiful photographs do not need study and explanation to give pleasure, and will nourish the growing interest in the subject with painlessly acquired information. We hope the already initiated will enjoy the faithful reproductions even more, knowing that the old, treasured nineteenth-century books with their handsome engravings are beyond the reach of the general public. Because of their great value, they usually are in the hands of private collectors and not available with sufficient ease even in the world's great libraries.

In the past three decades, Japan has become an increasingly popular source of inspiration (especially in the United States) for new approaches to modern living—Japanese country houses, gardens, flower arranging, cooking, and love of nature. Japanese civilization has never lost close contact with the wonders of the underwater world, possibly because Japan is a belt of small islands. The Japanese are keen observers of nature and no doubt owe much of their able craftsmanship to this national characteristic, copying from their earliest beginnings the miraculous constructions of the sea.

In any case, shell collecting has never lost its prestige there. The emperor is the owner of the nation's greatest shell collection, and one of the rarest Japanese shells is still known as the Emperor Shell (plate 1), so called because it is said that until recently every fisherman who found one had orders to deliver it to the only person entitled to own it—the emperor. The fierce competition in shell collecting remains, even though collecting is no longer reserved for the wealthy or titled. Collecting shells is the preoccupation of many humble Japanese, some of whom in time become experts to consult in cases of doubt over classification of certain rare specimens, a situation that frequently arises in conchological circles.

It does not seem pure coincidence that the process of producing a true pearl artificially was invented by Baron Mikimoto. Through his endless experimental efforts he obtained out of a living oyster shell this rare and precious jewel of the sea—a most complicated and well-organized manipulation. Step by step, his method led to a pearl of the greatest beauty and perfection. If he did not foresee the sweep of enthusiasm that would greet his discovery, he nevertheless must have been convinced from the beginning that his sophisticated effort to make nature let herself be used to work for the desires of man had every chance of success. (Incidentally, some of our Mississippi tributary sweet-water shells furnish the Japanese with the most suitable material for their purpose.) The nacreous shells are ground by enormous machines to exactly the right proportions. The dextrous, diligent, and ambitious Japanese were able to pool their efforts into workable organizations after the initial discovery of the proper methods. They were sensitive enough to understand and respect nature as a practical teacher and so to the greatest extent have been responsible for the formidable success of the cultured pearl.

Japanese shell devotees have found an original way to enhance the pleasure of owning and displaying their treasures. They exhibit a single shell, placing it before them; the small circle of shell devotees contemplates its particular beauty, shape, and artful design. The session is called "inspiration," and each participant expresses his own visual experience by comparing the shell to another object, abstract form, or animal: a bird, a storm cloud, a dragon, a favorite feminine hairdo. Their admiration grows with the variety of other aspects of life they find comparable to the architecture of the shell.

A friend of ours, when in New York, visited our shell exhibition and acquired a perfect specimen of a murex with the poetic name Comb of Venus (which it fully deserves). Its long graceful spines are curved slightly upward, giving it the likeness of a windswept wheat field bent rythmically for a fleeting moment. The shell retains its wondrous shape forever, as if the wind and the waves had permanently impressed the beauty of their own passing movements on its surface (plate 59). Our friend, one of the world's leading malacologists, later described to us how he and another friend who shares his interests had spent an evening in their hotel room acquainting themselves with the new addition to his collection. The weird and complicated structure invited comparison to other forms with which they were familiar in their daily lives. They imagined objects influenced by their worldly environment and in accord with their scientifically educated minds, certainly different ones from those of which the Japanese collectors were reminded. But the challenge of the shell remains the same, its code unbroken, stimulating the beholder to find at least a playful solution to the great mystery that surrounds the source of its creation.

Shells are the protective cases formed by mollusks. Basically limy in composition, they are usually in one or two parts. Univalves (plates 1–146) are gastropods (from the Latin meaning "stomach-foot"), and have a single shell, usually spirally coiled. In certain instances, some species are further protected by a plate (sometimes vestigial) called an operculum, which forms a sort of trapdoor that shields the animal after it withdraws into its shell. Bivalves (plates 147–184) live within two valves (or shell plates), which are joined by a hinge and a horny ligament. Bivalves protect themselves by closing their shells and have no operculum. Cephalopods (from the Latin meaning "head-foot") include the squid, octopus, cuttlefish, nautilus (plates 185, 186), and argonaut (plate 187). Except for the nautiluses, these have no external shells. Chitons (plate 188) have eight segmented plates, which are embedded in a belt of muscular tissue.

PLEUROTOMARIIDAE

PLATE 1 (*in color*)
(with mirror image)
Pleurotomaria hirasei Pilsbry   3 to 5″
Emperor's Slit Shell

Deep-water slit shells belong to the Pleurotomariidae, one of the rarest shell families. Formerly thought to be extinct, the family is now known to comprise twelve living species. The slit in the shell is used as a vent for the passage of sea water and waste materials. The Emperor's Slit Shell, the most common of the group, is found in the waters off Japan at a depth of about 300 feet.

HALIOTIDAE

PLATE 2
[*left*] *Haliotis rufescens* Swainson   10 to 12″
Red Abalone
[*right*] *Haliotis fulgens* Philippi   6 to 10″
Green Abalone

The abalone has a large muscular foot which it uses to cling tenaciously to rocks, and even the heaviest surf cannot dislodge it. The holes in the shells are used to expel sea water, which is drawn in under the shell, passed over the gills, and then forced out through the holes. The foot of the Abalone is considered a great delicacy by gourmets, and the beautiful iridescent shell linings are used widely in jewelry making.

The Red Abalone is one of the largest of the family, with a shell often attaining twelve inches across its widest part. The interior of its shell is nacreous, with a reddish cast. The Green Abalone has a greenish interior. Both are found off the California coast.

ACMAEIDAE and FISSURELLIDAE

PLATE 3

Limpets are low, very wide-mouthed univalves belonging to the family Acmaeidae. Most cling by a strong foot to rocks, but some are known to attach to seaweed. Keyhole limpets are of the family Fissurelli-

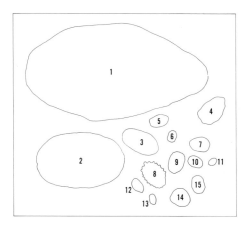

dae. They resemble true limpets, but have a hole, used for excretion, at the top of their shell.

[1] *Patella mexicana* Broderip and Sowerby   8 to 14″

Native to the west coast of the Americas, from the Gulf of California to Peru, this is the largest of the Acmaeidae. The specimen illustrated is covered with a downy coating of seaweed.

[2] *Megathura crenulata* Sowerby   3 to 5″
Giant Keyhole Limpet

This keyhole limpet is found on the coast of southern California and as far south as northern Lower California.

[3 and 4] *Fissurella barbadensis* Gmelin   1 to 1½″
Barbados Keyhole Limpet

The exterior of this shell varies in color from light gray to pink, and the neutral interior is bordered by a band of olive green. It is common to Florida and the West Indies.

[5] *Fissurella fascicularis* Lamarck   ¾ to 1¼″
Wobbly Keyhole Limpet

The narrow end of this keyhole limpet is raised, and if placed on a flat surface, the shell will rock. Thus it is known commonly as "wobbly." It is native to the West Indies, and especially common in Puerto Rico.

[6–15] Various limpets

The shells with holes are keyhole limpets; those without are true limpets.

ANGARIIDAE

PLATES 4 and 5

Angaria melanacantha Reeve   2½ to 3"
Imperial Delphinula

Both the spiny exterior and the nacreous aperture of this dark, purplish-brown shell are shown in these enlarged photographs. The Imperial Delphinula is a coral dweller and native to Philippine waters.

TROCHIDAE

PLATE 6 (*in color*)

Tegula regina Stearns   2"

Queen Tegula has a dark, spiral operculum and a brilliantly colored aperture. It is found in the deep waters off the coast of southern California.

TURBINIDAE

There are some five hundred species of Turbinidae, including the common star, turban, and pheasant shells. They have a hard, limy operculum, which in certain cases is deeply grooved.

PLATE 7

Astraea undosa Wood   2 to 3"

Found in shallow water on the coast of southern California and as far south as Lower California, this shell lives covered with a heavy, dark-brown periostracum, or outer skin.

PLATE 8

[*left*] *Astraea heliotropium* Martyn (underside) 3 to 4"

[*right*] *Astraea undosa* Wood (underside)   2 to 3"

PLATE 9 (*in color*)

Astraea heliotropium Martyn (operculum, 1")

This purplish-pink star shell is native to the waters around New Zealand. Its operculum is even more dramatic, and has all the brilliance of iridescent stained glass.

This greatly enlarged photograph displays the operculum's extraordinary complexity and its iridescent colors.

PLATE 10 (*in color*)

[*top three specimens*] *Turbo petholatus* Linné   2 to 3"
Tapestry Turban

During World War II, many United States servicemen stationed in the Pacific fashioned rings and jewelry from the shiny blue-green "cat's eye" that is the operculum of *Turbo petholatus*. This common shallow-water shell from the coral reefs of the South Pacific is extremely variable in color and pattern.

[*bottom*] *Turbo fluctuosus* Wood   1½ to 2″

This shell is native to the west coast of the Americas from Lower California to Peru. It has a sculptured operculum (plate 11) and is found in many color variations.

PLATE 11 (*in color*)
Turbo fluctuosus Wood (operculum)

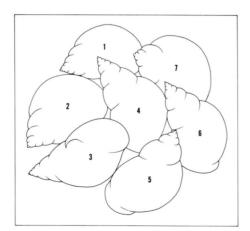

PLATE 12 (*in color*)
[*1–6*] *Phasianella australis* Gmelin   2 to 3″

There are some forty known species of pheasant shells (genus *Phasianella*), which take their name from the resemblance of their shells to the coloring and patterns of a pheasant's plumage. The largest, *Phasianella australis,* from southern Australia, is extremely varied in its surface decoration.

[*7*] *Phasianella ventricosa* Swainson   1 to 2″

Very close in appearance to *Phasianella australis* is *Phasianella ventricosa,* also from southern Australia. This shell is from deeper water than the former, and is slightly smaller and less elongated.

PLATE 13 (*in color*)
Phasianella australis Gmelin   2 to 3″

3

8

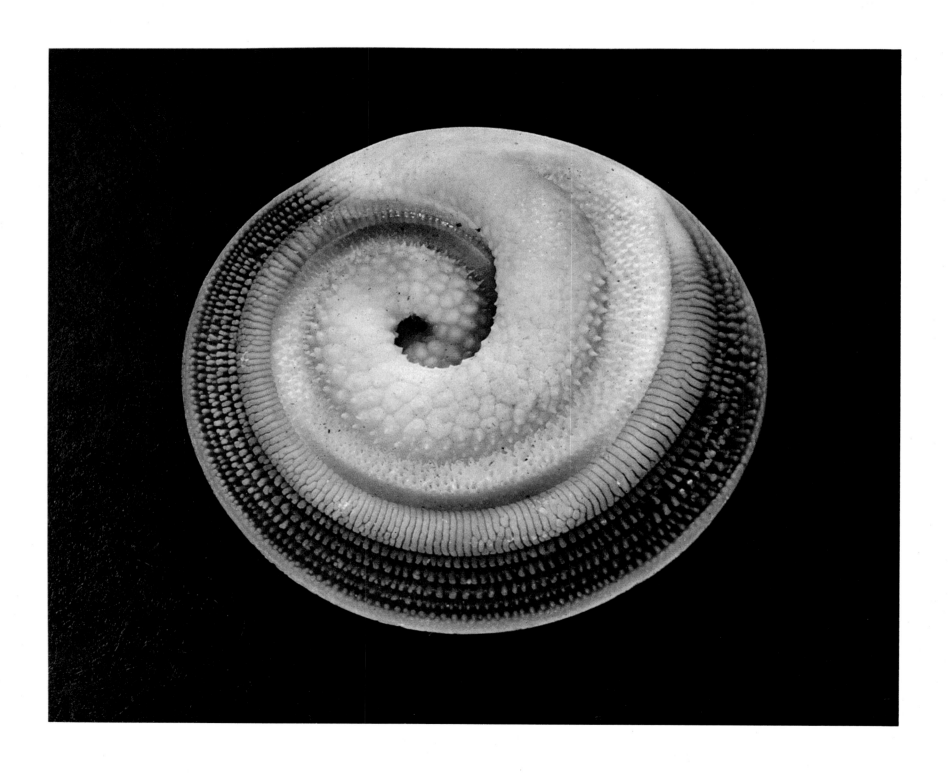

TURRITELLIDAE

PLATE 14

Turritella terebra Linné   3 to 5″
Auger Turritella

This auger-shaped Indo-Pacific species, with its regularly enlarging progression of multiple whorls, belongs to the Turritellidae. It is found in the tropics, on muddy bottoms in shallow water.

VERMETIDAE

PLATE 15

Vermicularia spirata Philippi   1 to 4″
Lady's Curl

These shells, from the tropical regions of the western Atlantic, would seem at first glance to be marine worms, although actually they are snails. In the young form, the shells resemble turritellas (plate 14), but as they mature they assume the haphazardly spiral formation seen here.

ARCHITECTONICIDAE

PLATES 16 and 17

Architectonica perspectiva Linné   1 to 2″
Perspective Sundial

The sundials are represented by some forty species, all native to tropical waters. They are characterized by extreme uniformity of appearance: small, low conical shells, decorated with slightly reticulated spiral bands. *Architectonica perspectiva* comes from the Indo-Pacific area, and has the typical clearly delineated design, beautiful coloration, and delicately sculptured surface (plate 16, greatly enlarged detail) and underside (plate 17).

CERITHIIDAE

PLATE 18

Cerithium fasciatum Bruguière   2 to 3″

Most of the approximately three hundred species of Cerithiidae inhabit shallow waters along tropical shores. The distinctively banded *Cerithium fasciatum* is found in the western Pacific, from northern Australia to Japan.

JANTHINIDAE

PLATE 19 (*in color*)

Janthina janthina Linné   1 to 1½″
Purple Sailor

Janthinas drift freely on the surface of tropical waters, kept afloat by a mass of mucus air bubbles attached to their foot. The purplish color camouflages the snail from the ocean birds above and from predatory fish below. Specimens are occasionally washed ashore during storms and afterward found in great numbers on beaches.

EPITONIIDAE

Over two hundred species of Epitoniidae inhabit the seas all over the world. The common name, "wentle-

trap," comes from the Dutch word meaning "spiral (or winding) staircase." Some species are extremely rare and have been prized collector's items for centuries.

PLATE 20

[1] *Epitonium magnificum* Sowerby   3 to 5″
Magnificent Wentletrap

This rare wentletrap is the largest of the Epitoniidae found in Japanese waters.

[2, 3, and 4] Epitonium scalare Linné   1 to 2½″
Precious Wentletrap

During the eighteenth century, this rare shell was considered the crowning glory of a European connoisseur's shell cabinet. *Epitonium scalare* is subtly colored: the whorls are a smooth, pale flesh-pink, and the ribs are whitish. Specimens are found from the China Sea to the coast of Queensland, Australia.

[5 and 6] Epitonium stigmaticum Pilsbry   ¾ to 1¼″
Stigmatic Wentletrap

These small shells are native to Japanese waters, where they are found at a depth of from 30 to 60 feet. Their all-over color, a creamy white, is delicately marked with brown spots (the "stigmata").

PLATE 21

Sthenorytis pernobilis Fischer and Bernardi   1 to 1½″
Noble Wentletrap

A most unusual and rare wentletrap, from southeast Florida and the Caribbean.

15

STROMBIDAE

The family Strombidae includes the true conchs, the spider conchs (genus *Lambis*), and tibia shells. True conchs are found throughout the world in warm waters; spider conchs, of which there are ten known species, are found only in the tropical Indo-Pacific. (Spider conchs are so named because of the spiderlike projections of their shells.) Tibia shells are deep-water shells from the central Pacific; they are all considered collector's items.

PLATE 22 (*in color*)
Strombus gallus Linné   4 to 6″
Rooster Conch

Underside and top of this fairly rare shell from the Caribbean.

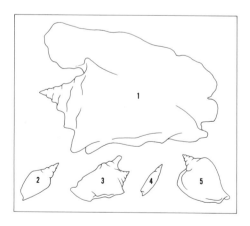

PLATE 23

[*1*] *Strombus gigas* Linné   8 to 10″
Queen Conch or Pink Conch

This is the typical conch that tourists bring back from the Caribbean. When found, the yellowish-brown periostracum is usually intact; when it is removed, the surface of the Queen Conch is whitish. The aperture is roseate, with subtle color gradations. In the West Indies, the natives employ the succulent flesh of the Queen Conch for their famous conch soup, and the shells are used as decorative edging for walks and garden paths.

[*2*] *Strombus vittatus japonicus* Reeve   2½″

Found in Japanese waters, this shell is a subspecies of the Pacific *Strombus vittatus* Linné.

[*3*] *Strombus raninus* Gmelin   2 to 4″
Hawkwing Conch

The common name of this Caribbean conch derives from its markings and the shape of its flaring mouth.

[*4*] *Terebellum terebellum* Linné   1 to 2″

The surface of this spindle-shaped shell is very smooth and shiny. Its color is almost white, and it is covered with light purplish-brown spots.

[*5*] *Strombus canarium* Linné   1½ to 4″

A common conch, this is found widely throughout the Indo-Pacific.

PLATE 24 (*in color*)
Lambis violacea Swainson   4″
Violet Spider Conch

One of the rare shells of the world, *Lambis violacea* is native to the waters surrounding the island of Mauritius. This specimen was taken alive by a scuba diver at a depth of 120 feet off the archipelago of Cargados, 300 miles northeast of Port Louis, Mauritius.

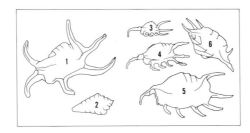

PLATE 25
[*1*] *Lambis chiragra* Linné   4 to 10″
Chiragra Spider Conch

[*2*] *Lambis chiragra* Linné   (immature form, 3″)

The immature *Lambis chiragra* lacks the characteristic spiny projections of the adult. The basic shape of the shell, however, is the same. This common spider conch is endemic to the southwest Pacific.

[*3*] *Lambis crocata* Link   4 to 5½″
Orange Spider Conch

An orange-colored aperture is typical of this uncommon shell. It has a wide range throughout the Indo-Pacific area, being found in shallow water from the east coast of Africa to Samoa, and from northern Australia to the Ryukyu Islands, Japan.

[*4*] *Lambis scorpius* Linné   4 to 6½″
Scorpion Conch

The aperture of the Scorpion Conch is striped with bands of purple and white. An uncommon shell, it is native to the tropical western Pacific.

[*5 and 6*] *Lambis lambis* Linné   4 to 8″
Common Spider Conch

The most common of all spider conchs, *Lambis lambis* is abundant throughout the Indo-Pacific area. Its inner construction may be seen in the cut specimen.

PLATE 26 (*in color*)
[*top*] *Tibia fusus* Linné   7 to 12″
Spindle Tibia

[*bottom left*] *Tibia powisi* Petit   1½ to 2″
Powis' Tibia

[*bottom right*] *Tibia martinii* Marrat   6″
Martini's Tibia

Tibia shells are deep-water shells from the central Pacific. They are all considered collector's items. This specimen of *Tibia fusus* was taken at a depth of 60 feet off Leyte Island, and the *Tibia martinii* was trawled in 120 fathoms off southern Luzon, in the Philippines. *Tibia powisi* is found from Japan to the southern Philippines.

PLATE 27 (*in color*)
Tibia fusus Linné   (enlarged detail)
Spindle Tibia

XENOPHORIDAE

Carrier shells (Xenophoridae) are low, conical shells with a broad base. They camouflage themselves by attaching pebbles, dead shells, and other detritus found on the ocean floor to the outer surface of their own shell. Those that collect shells are sometimes called "conchologists" and those that collect pebbles, "geologists."

PLATE 28, and PLATES 29 and 30 (*in color*)
Xenophora pallidula Reeve   2 to 4″
Japanese Carrier Shell

   Xenophora pallidula is native to the seas around Japan (specimens such as that in plate 29 have been collected as far away as Palawan Island in the Philippines) at depths of from 50 to 150 feet. Although carrier shells attach only dead material to their own shell, living ocean dwellers, such as the sponge (plate 28), coral (plate 29), or worm cases (plate 30) grow naturally on the already-attached dead shells.

PLATE 31 (*in color*)
Xenophora robusta Verrill   4″
Robust Carrier Shell

   So many dead shells have been fastened onto this *Xenophora robusta,* from Mexico's west coast, that the shell itself is hardly visible at all.

PLATE 32 (*in color*)
(with mirror image)
[*left*] *Xenophora exutus* Reeve   3 to 4″.

   A carrier shell from the western Pacific, *Xenophora exutus* is thin and fragile. If it does any collecting at all, it is only to the extent of cementing a few grains of fine sand to itself near the apex.

[*right*] *Xenophora peroniana* Iredale   2″

   The pebbled ocean floor in the deep waters off New South Wales, Australia, is the home of the *Xenophora peroniana.* It cements small stones to its own shell, thereby achieving an almost impenetrable shield and perfect camouflage. The order and precision with which this is done is indeed remarkable.

23

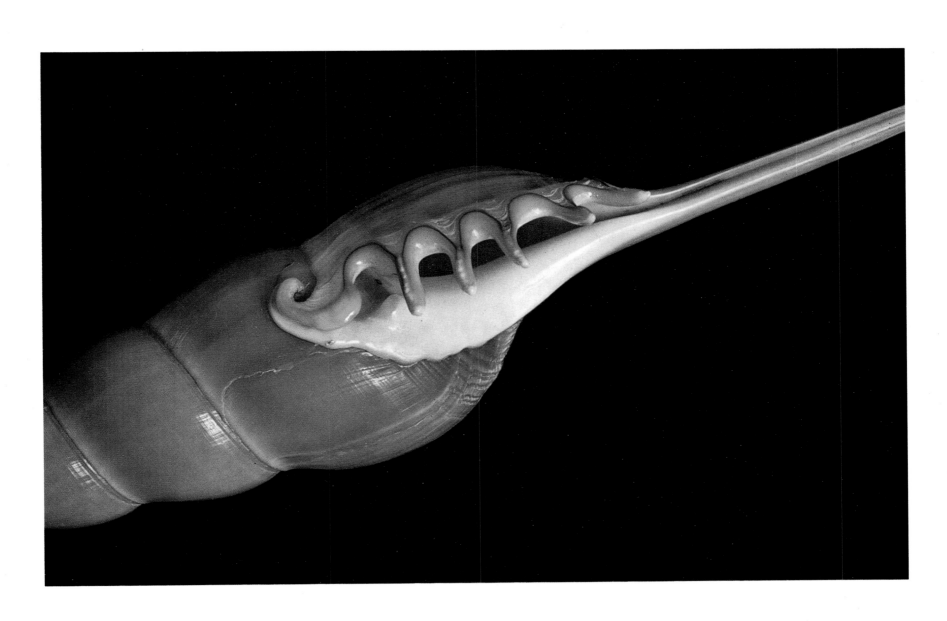

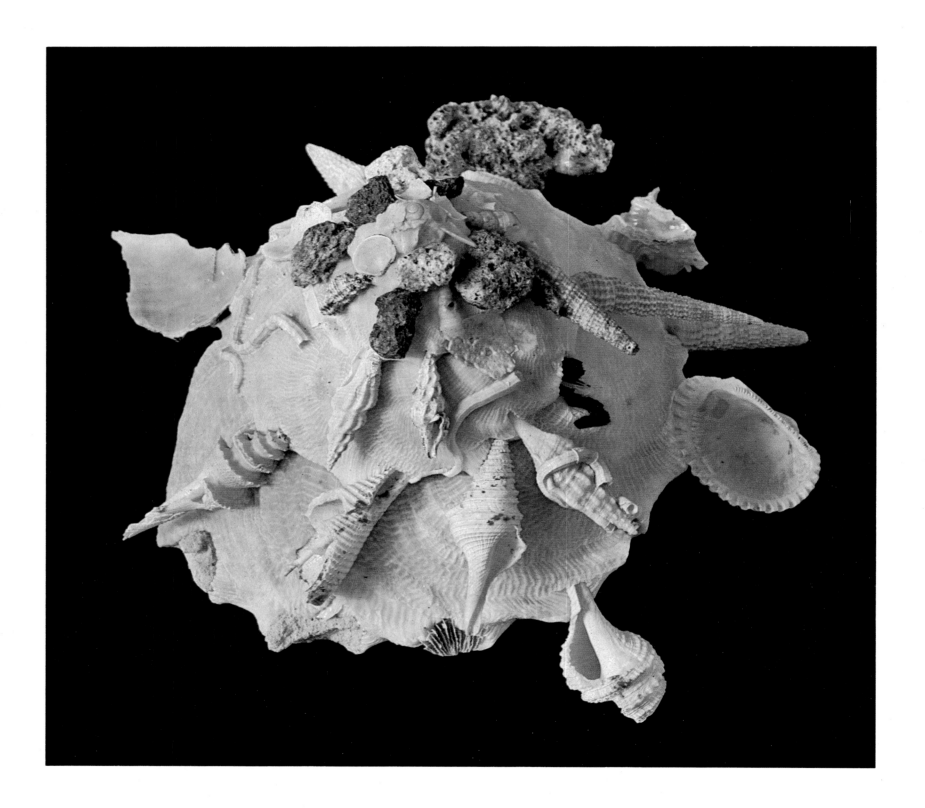

NATICIDAE

Naticas are world-wide in distribution and are found on sandy tidal flats. They are characterized by a generally smooth shell with few whorls, the one terminating in the aperture increasing in size quite abruptly.

PLATE 33
Polinices mammilla Linné 1½″

From the Philippines, this shell has an orange-yellow coloration.

OVULIDAE

The shells of the family Ovulidae are closely related to the cowries. They may be globular or beak- or spindle-shaped. There is much variety in their size and coloration.

PLATE 34 (*in color*)
[*top*] *Volva volva* Linné 3 to 5″
Shuttlecock

A common western-Pacific shell, this specimen is from the deep waters of the Torres Strait, between Australia and New Guinea.

[*bottom left*] *Volva brevirostris rosea* A. Adams
1 to 2″

This shell, from the western Pacific, is usually of a deep rose color, but it may be found in other hues as well.

[*bottom center*] *Volva birostris* Linné 1½ to 3″

A rare shell found in Japanese waters and southward to Malaysia.

[*bottom right*] *Neosimnia catalinensis* Berry ¾″

Deep water along the coast of southern California is the home of this delicate shell. The specimen illustrated was dredged in 300 feet of water off Carpinteria, near Santa Barbara.

PLATE 35
Ovula ovum Linné 2 to 4″

This glossy white shell with its dark interior is common throughout the Indo-Pacific area and has long been used by the native peoples as an amulet or charm.

CYPRAEIDAE

Usually ovoid in shape, cowries display a remarkable range of color and markings, from the palest tones to the deepest mottlings. The surface of the shell is usually highly polished and porcelainlike. Because of their shape and beauty, cowries have been employed by many tribes and civilizations throughout the world as religious fetishes, currency, and as objects of personal adornment. There are over two hundred species of cowries. They are among the most widely collected of all shells.

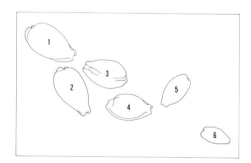

PLATE 36 (*in color*)

[*1 and 2*] *Cypraea saulae* Gaskoin   ¾ to 1″
Saul's Cowrie

The distribution of this rare shell is fairly wide,

from the central Philippines to Queensland, Australia. Despite variations in shells from different locations, all specimens of *Cypraea saulae* have one similar feature—a design at its center that resembles a freely brushed Oriental character. Chinese collectors affirm that the shell is popular with them because of this seeming abstraction of their calligraphy.

[*3*] *Cypraea walkeri bregeriana* Crosse   1″
Walker's Cowrie

This shell is found in the waters around New Caledonia.

[*4*] *Cypraea stolida* Linné   1 to 1½″
Stolid Cowrie

Several varieties of *Cypraea stolida,* some considered subspecies, are found throughout the Indo-Pacific area. This specimen is from Palawan Island in the Philippines.

[*5*] *Cypraea coxeni hesperina* Schilder and Summers ¾″

This shell is native to the warm waters surrounding the island of New Britain.

[*6*] *Cypraea punctata* Linné   ⅓ to ½″
Punctate Cowrie

An uncommon shell, distributed widely in the Indo-Pacific region.

PLATE 37 (*in color*)

(with mirror image)

[*left*] *Cypraea fultoni* Sowerby   2 to 2½″
Fulton's Cowrie

[*right*] *Cypraea hirasei* Roberts   2 to 2½″

Both specimens are in the collection of the Academy of Natural Sciences of Philadelphia. The very rare Fulton's Cowrie is found in the waters off South Africa. This one came from the stomach of a fish that feeds on it. *Cypraea hirasei,* from the Pacific coast of the Japanese island of Honshu, is apparently far rarer than most shell literature indicates.

PLATE 38 (*in color*)

[*1*] *Cypraea decipiens* E. A. Smith   2″
Decipiens Cowrie

A species found in the waters of Western Australia, this unusually dark specimen comes from Roebuck Bay, near Broome.

[*2*] *Cypraea thersites* Gaskoin   3″
Thersite Cowrie

Cypraea thersites resembles the usual variety of *decipiens,* although it is larger, lighter in color, and has a white border around its aperture. The shell seems to inhabit the entire southern coast of Australia and is

found as far north as Perth, in Western Australia, where this specimen was taken.

[*3*] *Cypraea pulchra* Gray   1¼ to 2″

This specimen comes from Muscat on the Gulf of Oman; the species ranges throughout the Indian Ocean.

[*4*] *Cypraea argus* Linné   2 to 4″
Eyed Cowrie

The early Italian sailors who first brought this shell from the Eastern oceans to Europe thought it looked so much like a little pig that they nicknamed it *porcellino* (piglet). In France, it became *porcelaine,* and it is still the French word for cowrie. Later, when glazed china was first imported to France from China, it too was called *porcelaine,* because the sheen of the china so

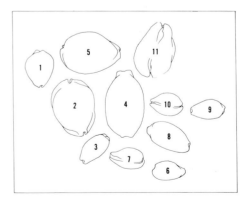

resembled that of the cowrie. *Cypraea argus* has a wide range in the Indo-Pacific area.

[5] *Cypraea mauritiana* Linné   2½ to 3½″
Humpback Cowrie

A common cowrie, *Cypraea mauritiana* is found throughout the Indo-Pacific area. Some specimens have a dark, purplish cast, which gives them a jewel-like quality.

[6] *Cypraea pyrum* Gmelin   1 to 1½″
Pear Cowrie

[7] *Cypraea pyrum* Gmelin   (underside)

The Mediterranean Sea and the coast of northeast Africa are the habitat of this shell.

[8] *Cypraea carneola* Linné   1 to 3″
Carnelian Cowrie

[9] *Cypraea onyx* Linné   1½″
Onyx Cowrie

These are common cowries native to the Indo-Pacific region.

[10] *Cypraea sulcidentata* Gray   1½″
Groove-Toothed Cowrie

This Hawaiian cowrie is distinctive because of the unusually long and well-defined grooves surrounding its aperture.

[11] *Cypraea stercoraria* Linné   2 to 3″
Rat Cowrie

Exceptionally well-defined teeth on the base are characteristic also of this cowrie, which is endemic to the west coast of tropical Africa.

PLATE 39 (*in color*)
(with mirror image)
Cypraea guttata Gmelin   2½″
Great Spotted Cowrie

This specimen of *Cypraea guttata*, one of only eighteen known in the world, is in the collection of the Academy of Natural Sciences of Philadelphia. It was found in the stomach of a fish caught off the Solomon Islands.

PLATE 40 (*in color*)
[*top*] *Cypraea venusta* Sowerby   2½ to 3″

This specimen was removed from sponge in 30 feet of water off Sorrento Reef, near Fremantle, Western Australia.

[*bottom left*] *Cypraea mappa* Linné   2½ to 3½″
Map Cowrie

The Indo-Pacific Map Cowrie, so called because of its maplike markings, is one of the world's most popular shells. Its light-brown shell often has a green tint in its shiny, porcelaneous surface. In the case of this unusual specimen, from the central Philippines, the green color predominates.

[bottom right] *Cypraea hesitata,* form *alba* Cox   4"
Umbilicate Cowrie

This rare white form of the common southern Australian *Cypraea hesitata* is found in very deep waters.

PLATE 41 (*in color*)
[left, top and bottom] *Cypraea aurantium* Gmelin
3 to 4"
Golden Cowrie

Until recent times, the Golden Cowrie was the royal symbol worn by Melanesian chiefs. It was believed that after death the soul took up residence in this shell. Fine examples have been found in the Philippine, Marshall, and Solomon Islands, but most come from treacherous coral reefs off the Fiji Islands.

[right] *Cypraea moneta* Linné   1"
Money Cowrie

For many centuries the Money Cowrie was used as currency in the Indo-Pacific, where it is a very common shell.

PLATES 42 and 43 (*in color*)
(with mirror image)
Cypraea mappa Linné   2½ to 3½"
Map Cowrie

This cowrie shows a lovely, slow spiral when cut crosswise (plate 42) and a very beautiful oval articulation when cut lengthwise (plate 43).

PLATE 44 (*in color*)
[left] *Cypraea friendii* Gray   2½ to 3"
Friend's Cowrie

Friend's Cowrie is found in the waters of Western Australia from Perth southward.

[right, top and bottom] *Cypraea tessellata* Swainson
1 to 2"
Tortoise Cowrie

The lustrous top and underside of this relatively rare Hawaiian cowrie are seen here.

PLATE 45 (*in color*)
[1] *Cypraea lynx* Linné   ¾ to 2"
Lynx Cowrie
[2] *Cypraea histrio* Gmelin   2 to 2½"
Histrio Cowrie

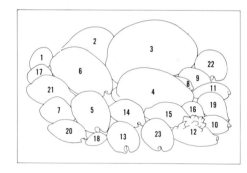

[3] *Cypraea tigris* Linné 2 to 4″
Tiger Cowrie

[4 and 5] *Cypraea talpa* Linné 2 to 3″
Mole Cowrie

[6] *Cypraea testudinaria* Linné 4 to 5″
Tortoise Cowrie

[7] *Cypraea depressa* Gray 1 to 1½″

[8] *Cypraea isabella* Linne 1″
Isabella Cowrie

[9 and 10] *Cypraea walkeri* Sowerby 1″
Walker's Cowrie

[11] *Cypraea onyx* Linné (immature specimen)
1 to 1½″
Onyx Cowrie

[12] *Cypraea erosa* Linné (with barnacles attached)
1 to 1¾″
Eroded Cowrie

[13] *Cypraea lamarcki* Gray 1½ to 2″
Lamarck's Cowrie

Native to the Indo-Pacific, these specimens give some idea of the great variety in the appearance of different species of cowries from a single area.

[14] *Cypraea eburnea* Barnes 1″

[15] *Cypraea subviridis* Reeve 1 to 1½″

Both shells are found in the southwestern Pacific and off the coast of Australia.

[16] *Cypraea moneta* Linné
Money Cowrie

An immature form of the Money Cowrie (plate 41 right).

[17] *Cypraea turdus* Lamarck 1 to 1½″
Thrush Cowrie

This common cowrie is found in the Indian Ocean.

[18] *Cypraea felina fabula* Kiener ½ to ¾″

Native to the northwestern Indian Ocean, this specimen came from the Bay of Muscat in the Gulf of Oman.

[19] *Cypraea pulchella* Swainson   1½″

This is a young specimen of a rare cowrie from Formosa.

[20] *Cypraea annettae* Dall   1 to 1½″

One of the few American cowries, this shell is found off the west coast of Mexico and Central America.

[21 and 22] *Cypraea spadicea* Swainson   1 to 2″
Chestnut Cowrie

This is the only cowrie native to the west coast of the United States. It is found off California from Monterey southward.

[23] *Cypraea zonaria* Linné   1 to 1½″

A richly mottled species found off the west coast of Africa.

PLATE 46 (*in color*)
(shown about twice actual size)

[1] *Cypraea helvola* Linné (immature specimen)   ½″
Honey Cowrie

[2] *Cypraea nucleus* Linné   ¾″
Nucleus Cowrie

[3] *Cypraea lutea* Gmelin   ½ to ¾″

[4] *Cypraea asellus* Linné   ½ to 1″
Little Donkey Cowrie

[5] *Cypraea clandestina* Linné   ½″

[6] *Cypraea cribraria* Linné   ¾ to 1″
Sieve Cowrie

[7] *Cypraea kieneri* Hidalgo   ¾″
Kiener's Cowrie

[8] *Cypraea hirundo* Linné   ½ to ¾″

[9] *Cypraea staphylaea* Linné   ¾″

[10] *Pustularia cicercula* Linné   ½″
Chickpea Cowrie

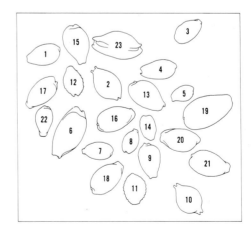

These shells from the Indo-Pacific are examples of the smaller species of cowries.

[11] *Trivia radians* Lamarck   ¾″

[12] *Jenneria pustulata* Lightfoot   ¾ to 1″

These cowries, along with *Cypraea nucleus* [2], are among the few with textured shells. Both are found off Mexico and as far south as Ecuador.

[13] *Cypraea diluculum* Reeve   ¾″

[14] *Cypraea fimbriata* Gmelin   ½″

Two species endemic to the east coast of Africa.

[15] *Cypraea coxeni* Cox ¾ to 1″
Cox's Cowrie

This uncommon cowrie is native to the waters of Melanesia.

[16] *Cypraea verconis* Cotton and Godfrey   ¾″

A cowrie native to South Australia.

[17] *Cypraea quadrimaculata* Gray   ¾″

This species is from the southwestern Pacific.

[18] *Cypraea ziczac* Linné   ½ to 1″
Zigzag Cowrie

[19] *Cypraea boivini* Kiener   1″
Boivin's Cowrie

[20] *Cypraea labrolineata* Gaskoin   ½ to 1″

Three cowries native to the western Pacific.

[21] *Cypraea gracilis* Gaskoin   ¾″
Graceful Cowrie

[22] *Cypraea gracilis japonica* Schilder   ½″
Graceful Cowrie

Cypraea gracilis is a common western-Pacific cowrie, while *japonica* is a subspecies abundant in the shallow waters of Japan. These typify the slight variations that separate one variety of shell from the next.

[23] *Cypraea limacina* Lamarck   ¾″

The underside of this white-spotted shell, native to the waters of Japan.

41

43

CASSIDAE

The family Cassidae includes both helmet and bonnet shells. The large helmets are found throughout the world in tropical waters, and are widely used in making cameos.

PLATE 47

Cassis cornuta Linné (aperture and top)   10 to 12″
Horned Helmet

This large helmet, Indo-Pacific in origin, is usually found in shallow water, partly buried in sand.

PLATE 48

[1] *Cassis madagascariensis* Lamarck   5 to 9″
Emperor or Queen Helmet

A large species found from southeast Florida to the West Indies. Its flesh is edible, and its shell is used for cameos.

[2] *Cassis tuberosa* Linné   5 to 9″
King Helmet

This shell is also used for cameos and its flesh is also edible. It is found along the southeast coast of the United States, in the Caribbean, and off South America.

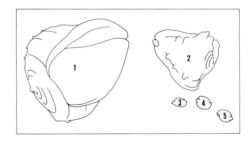

[3] *Casmaria erinaceus* Linné   1½ to 2″

This shell can show an extremely wide variation in color, shape, and markings. It is found throughout the Indo-Pacific.

[4 and 5] *Phalium bisulcatum* Schubert and Wagner   2″

One of the many bonnet shells, this species is common throughout the Indo-Pacific area. The pair shown here typify its wide variations of marking and coloration.

PLATE 49

[*top left*] *Phalium granulatum* Born   1½ to 3″
Scotch Bonnet

A shell found commonly along the beaches of the southeastern United States and the West Indies.

[*bottom left*] *Phalium glaucum* Linné   3 to 4″
Gray Bonnet

An unusual blue-gray color is characteristic of this Indo-Pacific shell.

[*top right*] *Cassis fimbriata* Q. and G.   2 to 3″

A bonnet shell which is endemic to South Australia, decorated with broad, wavy brown vertical stripes and narrow horizontal lines.

[*bottom right*] *Phalium strigatum* Gmelin   2 to 3″
Striped Bonnet

One of the most common Asiatic members of the Cassidae family.

CYMATIIDAE

The tritons, all members of the family Cymatiidae, are among the largest gastropods in existence and some-times reach a length of more than sixteen inches. Most are found in tropic waters near coral reefs. The Triton Trumpets comprise fewer than a dozen species, and are all equipped with horny opercula. The Hairy Tritons comprise about fifty species and are called "hairy" because their periostracum is covered with hairlike strands. Tritons, the trumpets of the mythological attendants of the ancient sea gods, have been used by many peoples as a musical instrument.

PLATE 50

[*left, and right top*] *Charonia tritonis* Linné   8 to 16″
Pacific Triton

The Pacific Triton has been used for millenniums in many parts of the world as a musical instrument for religious and martial occasions. When its tip is cut off and a mouthpiece attached, it produces an eerie sound when blown. It is found in the Indo-Pacific. This species is especially notable for its markings: a partridge pattern in shades of brown ranging from deep chocolate to pink. The small specimen displays the same proportions and markings.

[*right bottom*] *Phanozesta semitorta* Kuroda and Habe
1½ to 2″

This species, one of the many small members of the Cymatiidae, is native to Japanese waters.

PLATE 51
Charonia tritonis Linné (aperture)
Pacific Triton

PLATE 52
Distorsio reticulata Röding   2 to 4″

Endemic to the waters of the Indo-Pacific region, this shell has wide, flesh-colored, heavily callused inner and outer lips.

PLATES 53 and 54
Cymatium spengleri Perry   3 to 6″

This Hairy Triton is found along the eastern coast of Australia, from southern Queensland to Victoria.

PLATE 55
Fusitriton oregonensis Redfield   4 to 6″

This beautifully proportioned white shell, shown covered with its hairy periostracum, ranges from Japan to the coast of North America from the Bering Sea to San Diego, California.

TONNIDAE

PLATE 56
[*left*] *Malea ringens* Swainson   4 to 7″
Grinning Tun
[*right*] *Tonna allium* Dillwyn   2½ to 5″
Onion Tun

Tun shells, of the family Tonnidae, take their common name from their resemblance to a tun (bulging wine cask). Native to the west coast of Mexico and southward to Peru, *Malea ringens* is the only tun shell found off the west coast of the Americas. *Tonna allium* is native to tropical Indo-Pacific waters. Its over-all color is white; light brown may occur along the ribs.

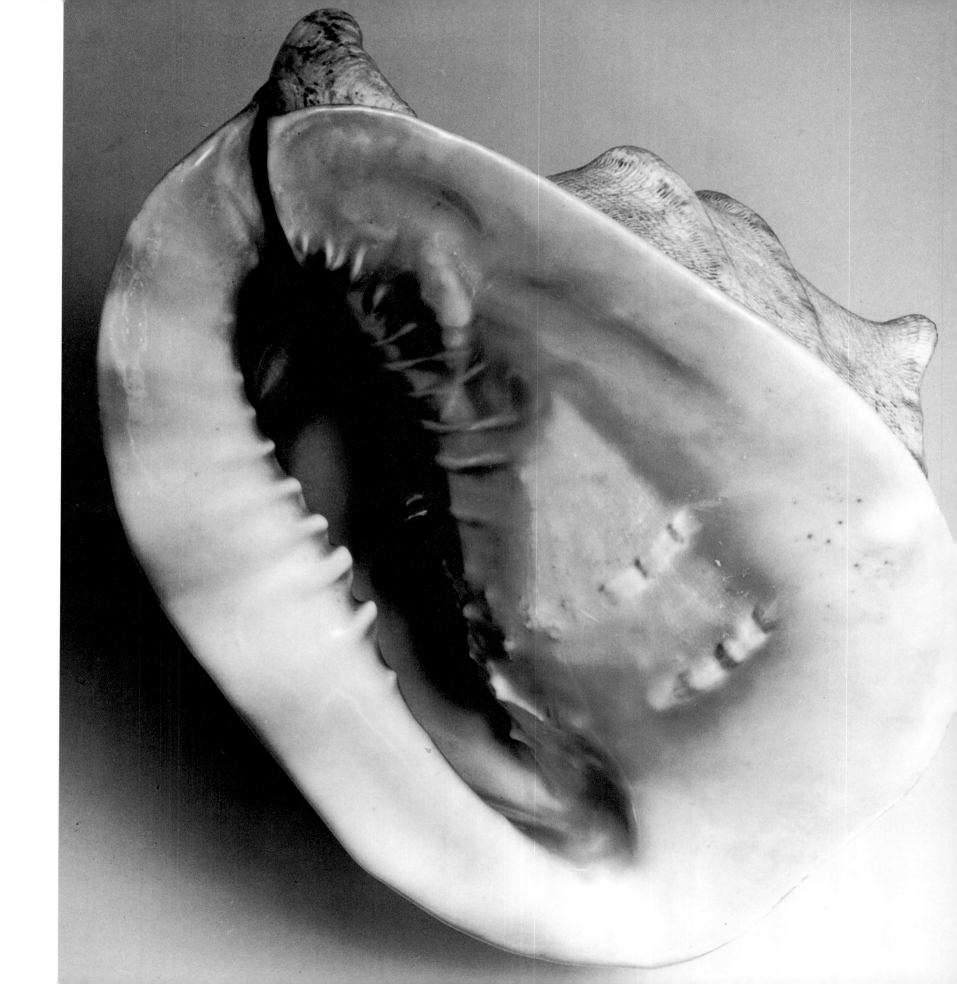

47

48

50

MURICIDAE

Murex shells are found all over the world, but are most prevalent in tropical waters. The most characteristic features of many of the Muricidae are the numerous spiny projections of their shells. The name murex, from the Latin meaning "purple fish," comes from the dye that was extracted from the Dye Murex (*Murex brandaris* Linné) by Mediterranean peoples more than three thousand years ago. The color, obtained by boiling a yellowish fluid secreted by the snails, was known as Royal Tyrian Purple.

PLATE 57 (*in color*)
[*left*] *Murex alabaster* Reeve 5″

This very rare and exquisite specimen was taken alive in 420 feet of water in Tosa Bay, Japan, and is now in the collection of the Academy of Natural Sciences of Philadelphia.

[*right*] *Murex cornucervi* Röding 3½ to 4½″

Long free-curving spines are characteristic of *Murex cornucervi*, which is native to the northern coast of Australia. This species was formerly known as *Murex monodon* Sowerby. (See also plates 65–67 and 69.)

PLATE 58 (*in color*)
Murex lobeckii Kobelt 2¼″
Lobeck's Murex

This specimen of the very rare *Murex lobeckii* was found in Tosa Bay, Japan. It is now in the collection of the Academy of Natural Sciences of Philadelphia.

PLATE 59
Murex pecten Lightfoot 4 to 6″
Comb of Venus

The Comb of Venus, with over one hundred perfectly arranged, needle-sharp spines, is a sand and rock dweller of the Indo-Pacific area. Though not uncommon, it is very difficult to obtain an absolutely perfect specimen. This species was formerly known as *Murex triremus* Perry.

PLATE 60
Murex zamboi Burch and Burch 1½ to 2½″

This species, a coral dweller, comes from the central Philippines.

PLATE 61 (*in color*)
[*left*] *Murex nigritus* Philippi 4 to 6″

This species inhabits the sandy flats of the Gulf of California.

[*right*] *Murex cabriti* Bernardi 2 to 3″
Cabrit's Murex

A prized collector's item from south Florida and the Caribbean.

PLATE 62 (*in color*)
[*left*] *Murex palmarosae* Lamarck   3 to 4″
Rose-branch Murex

This shell with its pink-tipped fronds is native to much of the tropic Indo-Pacific area. Some of the most beautiful examples come from Ceylonese waters.

[*right*] *Murex saulii* Sowerby   3 to 4″
Saul's Murex

The specimen shown here is an unusual color form of the Indo-Pacific *Murex saulii,* a close relative of the more frequently seen *Murex palmarosae.* It was taken off Palawan Island in the Philippines.

PLATE 63

Murex cervicornis Lamarck   1½ to 2½″

Two views of this northeast Australian species, covered with curved, hornlike projections.

PLATE 64

[*top left*] *Murex tripterus* Born   1½ to 2½″

A rare Indo-Pacific coral dweller, this specimen is from the waters off Bohol Island in the central Philippines.

[*top right*] *Murex vespertilio* Kira   1 to 2″

This slender shell from Japan is light brown and marked with darker brown spots.

[*bottom*] *Murex bipinnatus* Reeve   1¼ to 2″

A western-Pacific murex that resembles the famed Clavus Murex (plate 78) but has a purple mouth. This specimen comes from the Philippines.

PLATES 65, 66, and 67

Murex cornucervi Röding   3½ to 4½″

Typical specimens of *Murex cornucervi* vary from dark brown to almost black (plate 67, right). Occasionally, however, a white form is found, such as is seen in plates 65 and 66.

PLATE 68

Murex scorpio Linné   1 to 2″
Scorpion Murex

Murex scorpio is a small, delicately sculptured, dark-brown or black shell from tropical Pacific waters. The white, or albino, form shown here is a rarity.

PLATE 69

Murex cornucervi Röding   1½ to 2″

This is a miniature form of the *Murex cornucervi* (plates 57, 65–67). Characteristic of the shell is the one longer spine, which often curves back far enough to touch the shell itself. The specimens shown here are from the Torres Strait off northern Australia.

PLATE 70

Murex axicornis Lamarck   1½ to 3″

These specimens of this tropical Indo-Pacific shell were found off northern Queensland, Australia.

PLATE 71

[*left*] *Murex mindanensis* Sowerby   3 to 4″

This specimen was trawled in the deep waters of Tayabas Bay, Luzon, the Philippines.

[*right*] *Murex beaui* Fischer and Bernardi   3 to 5″

An uncommon species of the Muricidae from deep waters off southern Florida, the Gulf of Mexico, and the Caribbean.

PLATES 72 and 73

Murex territus Reeve   2½ to 3″

Two views of this specimen from Keppel Bay, Queensland, Australia.

PLATE 74

Murex cichoreus Gmelin   2½ to 3″
Endive Murex

The albino form of a common black-and-white Indo-Pacific coral-reef dweller.

PLATE 75

[*left*] *Murex tweedianus* Macpherson   2 to 3″

This murex is from the area of Queensland, Australia.

[*right*] *Murex hirasei* Hirase   1½ to 3″

Found in deep waters off Japan, this rare shell has brown, striated markings.

PLATE 76

[*left*] *Murex haustellum* Linné   3 to 6″
Snipe's Bill Murex

A moderately common murex in the Indo-Pacific, this species lives in pairs in fairly deep water.

[*right*] *Murex stainforthi* Reeve   1½ to 3″

A moderately common species from northwestern Australia.

PLATE 77

[*left*] *Murex senegalensis* Gmelin   1½ to 2″

This shell has been found in tropical waters on both sides of the Atlantic—off the coasts of Senegal and Brazil.

[*right top*] *Murex sobrinus* A. Adams   1½ to 2″

A light-brown shell marked with two dark-brown spiral bands, this murex inhabits moderately deep waters off Japan.

[*right bottom*] *Murex elenensis* Dall   1½ to 2″

This shell is found along the west coast of the Americas from Mexico to Peru.

PLATE 78
Murex elongatus Lightfoot   2 to 4″
Clavus Murex

These two specimens of the rare Indo-Pacific Clavus Murex were taken in the waters off Bohol Island in the central Philippines.

PLATE 79 (*in color*)
[*left, top and bottom*] *Pterorytis foliata* Gmelin
1½ to 3½″
Leafy Purpura

Native to the west coast of North America, this shell is found from San Diego, California, to Alaska. These two specimens were caught in 100 feet of water off San Diego.

[*right*] *Murex macropterus* Deshayes   1½ to 3″

Normally over-all brown in color, *Murex macropterus* is occasionally found with stripes, as seen in this specimen, which was taken by a diver in 90 feet of water off Santa Cruz Island, southern California.

PLATE 80 (in color)
(with mirror image)
Murex steeriae Reeve   3½″

One of the rare murices in the collection of the Academy of Natural Sciences of Philadelphia, this specimen is from the Marquesas Islands.

PLATE 81
Forreria belcheri Hinds   3 to 6″

This murex is native to shallow waters off southern California and Lower California.

PLATES 82 and 83
Forreria cerrosensis Dall   1½ to 2″

This uncommon species of murex is found in fairly deep water in the southern half of the Gulf of California and along the west coast of Mexico as far south as Acapulco.

PLATE 84
Concholepas concholepas Bruguière   4 to 5″
Barnacle Rock Shell

As with the abalone, which this rock shell resembles, the broad aperture enables the foot to get a firm hold on rocks that are exposed to the heavy pounding of the surf. It is native to the rocky shores of Chile and Peru, and its flesh is commonly used as food. This member of the Muricidae is very often found covered with barnacles, as is the case with the specimen on the right.

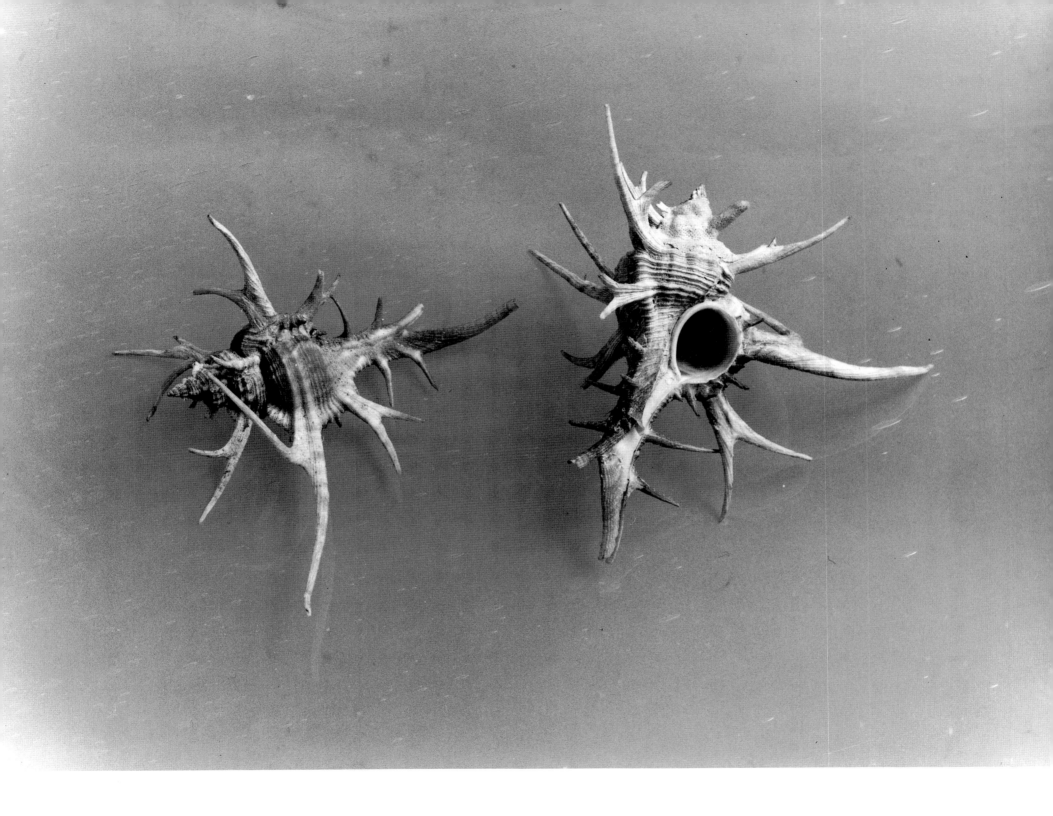

MAGILIDAE

Latiaxis, rapa, and coral shells are members of the family Magilidae. Latiaxis shells are deep-water dwellers, notable for their alabaster-white coloration and their delicately sculptured shapes. Rapa shells usually live near, and often within, soft corals on reefs in warm and shallow tropic waters. Certain species are found, however, in deep water. Rapas are usually small and whitish, with fragile, translucent globular shells. Coral shells, so called because they are coral dwellers, are found in the tropic seas of both hemispheres.

PLATES 85 and 86
[*left in each plate*] *Latiaxis mawae* Griffith and Pidgeon   1½ to 2″
Mawe's Latiaxis

[*right in each plate*] *Latiaxis lischkeanus* Dunker
1 to 2″
Lischke's Latiaxis

Apex and aperture views of two Japanese latiaxis shells, illustrating their unique appearance. *Latiaxis mawae* is the largest among the Japanese coral dwell-

ers. The *Latiaxis lischkeanus* illustrated here was taken at a depth of over 900 feet in Tosa Bay, Japan.

PLATE 87
Latiaxis idoleum Jonas   1 to 2″
Queen Eugenia's Latiaxis

The graceful Queen Eugenia's Latiaxis is a small white shell, native to very deep water in the seas off Japan.

PLATE 88
[*left*] *Latiaxis winckworthi* Fulton   1 to 2″
Winckworth's Latiaxis

[*top*] *Latiaxis kinoshitai* Fulton   1 to 1½″
Kinoshita's Latiaxis

[*bottom*] *Latiaxis tosanus* Hirase   1″
Tosa Latiaxis

[*right*] *Latiaxis pilsbryi* Hirase   1″
Pilsbry's Latiaxis

Four examples of latiaxis shells from the waters around Japan.

PLATE 89

[left] *Latiaxis kawamurai* Kira   1″
Kawamura's Latiaxis

[top] *Latiaxis deburghiae* Reeve (rough form)   1″

[bottom] *Latiaxis deburghiae* Reeve (smooth form) 1″
Miss de Burgh's Latiaxis

[right] *Latiaxis kiranus* Kuroda   1″
Kira's Latiaxis

Four other varieties of latiaxis shells from Japan, showing the variations to be found in shells from the same family and area.

PLATE 90 (*in color*)

[left] *Coralliophila pyriformis* Kira   1″

This coral dweller, usually found around Japanese waters, was taken from a depth of 100 feet off northeast Australia.

[right] *Latiaxis spinosus* Hirase   1″
Spinose Latiaxis

One of the more common species of the delicate Japanese Latiaxis.

PLATE 91

Rapa rapa Linné   2 to 3″
Papery Rapa

This species inhabits soft coral in the waters off the southern Philippines. Because it lives within the coral, it is almost impossible to find specimens *in situ*. They are generally collected after being washed up on beaches. In its immature form, as seen at right, *Rapa rapa* displays a longer siphonal canal with a proportionately smaller last whorl.

BUCCINIDAE

Whelks belong to the family Buccinidae and comprise a group of more than four hundred species. They are among the few mollusk families with a range that extends from arctic to tropic waters. The cold-water species are dull in color, while the warm-water ones are generally very colorful.

PLATE 92

[top] *Busycon contrarium* Conrad   4 to 16″
Lightning Whelk

This species normally is sinistral—its whorls descend in a counterclockwise spiral as opposed to the clockwise direction of almost all other shells (except in rare, atypical cases). It is common to the southeast coast of the United States and the northern portion of the Gulf of Mexico.

[*bottom left*] *Neptunea decemcostata* Say   3 to 4″
New England Neptune

A common cold-water shell found offshore, from the coast of Massachusetts to Labrador.

[*bottom center*] *Buccinum adelphicus* Dall   3 to 4″

A deep-water shell with extremely handsome markings and whorls that is native to Japan's Pacific coast.

[*bottom right*] *Busycon candelabrum* Lamarck
4 to 6″

A beautifully formed spiral shell found off the coast of Yucatan.

PLATES 93 and 94
Buccinum tenuissimum Taki   5 to 7″

This whelk is native to deep waters off the north coast of the island of Honshu, Japan. Its flesh is highly prized by Japanese gourmets.

PLATE 95
[*1, 2, and 3*] *Syrinx aruanus* Linné   12 to 24″
Australian Trumpet Shell

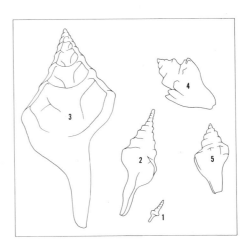

The world's largest univalve, sometimes attaining a length of over two feet, *Syrinx aruanus* is native to the waters of northern Australia, from the most westerly point all the way to the Great Barrier Reef. The juvenile shell [1] remains as the apex of the young shell [2] and then is usually broken off in the mature shell, shown here in cross section [3].

[4] *Volema pugilina* Born   4 to 5″

This Indo-Pacific shell is extremely heavy for its size. The specimen shown here is from off Darwin, Australia.

This South Atlantic shell is found in the waters of tropical western Africa and Brazil.

[5] *Hemifusus morio* Linné   3½ to 5″

This South Atlantic shell is found in the waters of tropical western Africa and Brazil.

FASCIOLARIIDAE

Fasciolariidae include the tulip shells of the southeastern United States, and spindle shells (genus *Fusinus*).

PLATE 96

Opeatostoma pseudodon Burrow   1½″

This odd member of the family Fasciolariidae is native to the west coast of the Americas from the Gulf of California to Peru. Characteristic of the species is the single long spinelike tooth on the lower part of the lip, which it uses for opening bivalves.

PLATE 97

[*left*] *Pleuroploca gigantea* Kiener   10 to 23″
Florida Horse Conch

Found along the southeast coast of the United States and in the Gulf of Mexico, the Horse Conch is the largest shell native to American waters.

[*right*] *Nassaria magnifica* Lischke   1 to 2″

This small shell is native to the deep waters off Japan, and is related to the buccinid whelks.

PLATE 98

[*left*] *Fusinus colus* Linné   4 to 7″
Distaff Spindle

Fusinus colus, an Indo-Pacific shell, lives on sandy bottoms and travels over the sand in pairs.

[*right*] *Fusinus eucosmius* Dall   2½ to 3″

This spindle shell is native to the Gulf of Mexico.

95

96

OLIVIDAE

Olive shells have the same shiny, porcelaneous surface as the cowries. They vary greatly in coloration and markings. They live in sandy bottoms in shallow water.

PLATE 99 (*in color*)
Oliva porphyria Linné (enlarged detail)   3 to 5″
Tent Olive

     The Tent Olive ranges from the Gulf of California to Panama.

PLATE 100 (*in color*)
[*left top*] *Baryspira albocallosa* Lischke   2½ to 3″

     Baryspira albocallosa is a deep-water shell native to Japan.
[*left bottom*] *Olivancillaria urceus* Röding   2½″
Brazilian False Olive

     A most unusual shell, found in shallow waters off the coast of Brazil.
[*right, top and bottom*] *Ancillista velesiana* Iredale
3 to 4″

     Ancillista velesiana is native to the coast of New South Wales, while similar species are found elsewhere in Australian waters. The young specimen (top) has not yet achieved its full, dark coloration.

MITRIDAE

The miters comprise over six hundred species native to tropic and semitropic waters. They are especially numerous in the Indo-Pacific. Miters grow in many different shapes; often the smaller ones resemble cones, olives, or true conchs.

PLATE 101
[*left*] *Mitra isabella* Swainson   2 to 4″
Isabel Miter

     A sand-colored miter from Japan.
[*right*] *Mitra belcheri* Hinds   4 to 5″
Belcher's Miter

     This deeply sculptured shell with a dark, almost black epidermis and a light-colored interior, ranges along the west coast of Central America from Mexico to Panama.

PLATE 102 (*in color*)
Mitra taeniata Lamarck   2 to 2½″

Northeast Australia is the native ground of the banded *Mitra taeniata*.

PLATE 103
[1] *Mitra glans* Reeve   1″
A miter shell from the Philippines.
[2] *Mitra exasperata* Gmelin   2″

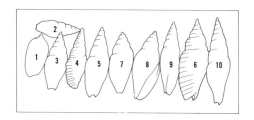

[3] *Mitra clathrus* Gmelin   1″
[4] *Mitra filaris* Linné   1″
[5] *Mitra papilio* Link   1 to 2″
[6] *Mitra granatina* Lamarck   1 to 2″
Examples of the numerous miter species of the Indo-Pacific.
[7 and 8] *Mitra hirasei* Pilsbry   1 to 2″
Two views of this small, basket-weave-patterned shell found off Japan.

[9] *Mitra granosa* Gmelin   1 to 2″
A miter native to the western Pacific.
[10] *Mitra caffer* Gmelin, form *formosensis* Sowerby 1 to 2″
A miter subspecies native to the area of Taiwan.

PLATE 104 (*in color*)
Mitra mitra Linné   3 to 5″
Episcopal Miter
A very common Indo-Pacific shell, the handsome Episcopal Miter dwells in coral reefs. This cut specimen shows its fascinating interior architecture.

VASIDAE

PLATE 105
Vases, belonging to the small family Vasidae, all live in tropic or subtropic waters.
[*left*] *Vasum muricatum* Linné   2½ to 4″
Caribbean Vase
A common shallow-water shell from southern Florida and the West Indies.
[*right*] *Tudicula armigera* A. Adams   2 to 3″
An uncommon shell found off the coast of northern Australia.

PLATE 106
Altivasum flindersi Verco 6″

This extremely rare shell—there are only about fifty collected specimens extant—was gathered at a depth of 600 feet in the waters of the Great Australian Bight, off the coast of South Australia. It is in the collection of the Academy of Natural Sciences of Philadelphia.

XANCIDAE

PLATE 107 (*in color*)
Xancus angulatus Lightfoot 8 to 10″
Lamp Chank

This shell is closely related to the Sacred Chank of India (*Xancus pyrum*), which the Hindus have given to the god Vishnu as one of his attributes. Native to the Caribbean, *Xancus angulatus* is a very heavy and massive shallow-water shell. Its common name derives from the fact that it was used by the natives of the West Indies as an oil lamp. The specimen pictured here has been cut to show its powerfully articulated interior structure.

HARPIDAE

The harp shells are limited to some twelve species, all native to tropical waters. Most are fairly common throughout the Indo-Pacific. Harp shells are noted for their extraordinarily rich color and markings, and for their deeply sculptured ribs.

PLATE 108 (*in color*)

[*top*] *Harpa davidis* Röding 2 to 4″
An uncommon shell with a wide distribution in the Indo-Pacific.
[*bottom, left and right*] *Harpa harpa* Linné 1½ to 2″
This shallow-water Indo-Pacific shell was formerly called *Harpa conoidalis* Lamarck.

PLATE 109 (*in color*)

Harpa costata Linné 2 to 3″
Imperial Harp
The aperture and top of the *Harpa costata*. This rare shell is the most sought-after harp among collectors. It is native to the Indian Ocean off the island of Mauritius.

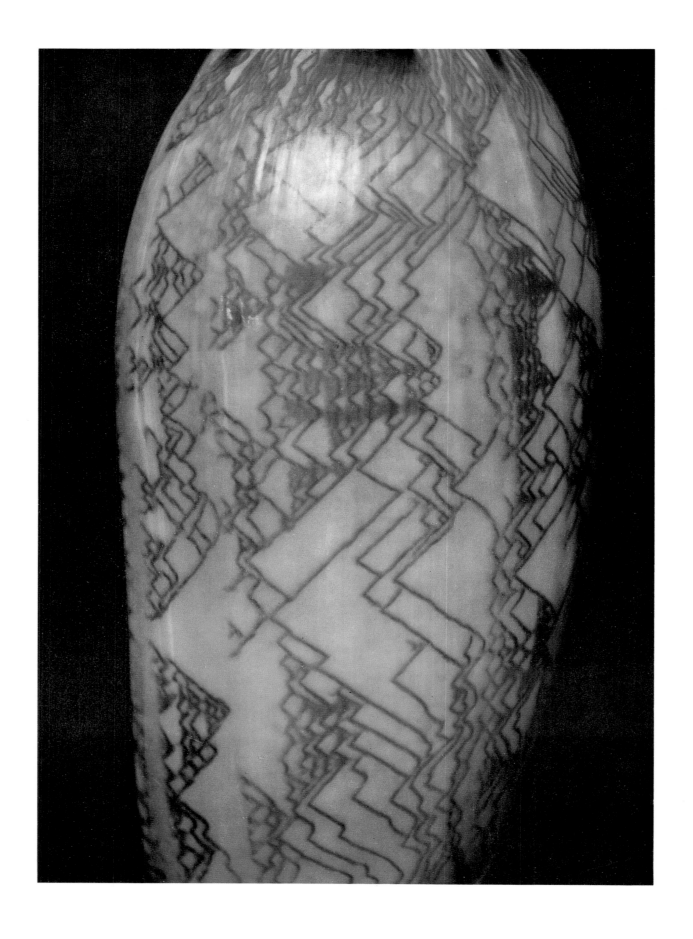

103

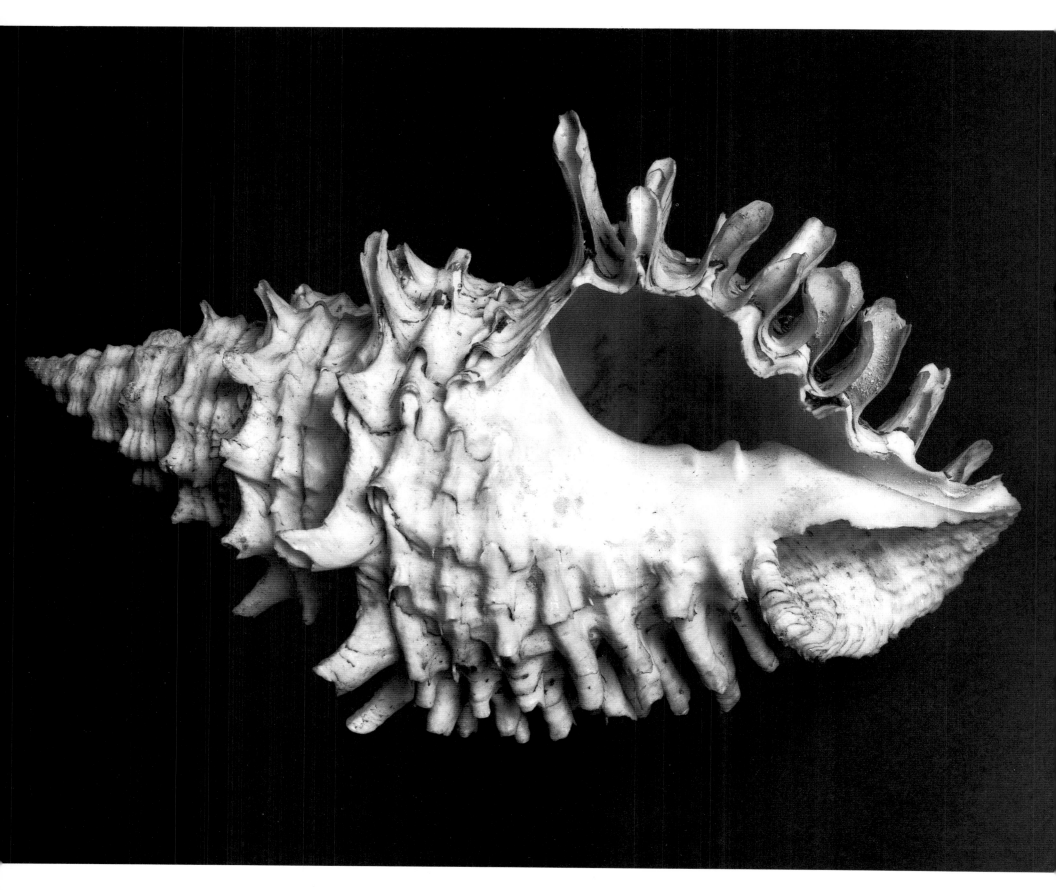

VOLUTIDAE

The Volutidae comprise a family of about two hundred different species, found throughout the world. Most inhabit shallow tropical waters, although some are deep-water dwellers and a few are found in arctic seas. Volutes are among the more mobile gastropods, and crawl about with considerable rapidity. Subfamilies include the Scaphellinae from the Caribbean area, some of which are extremely rare and all of which are notable for their superb markings. The bailer shells, native to the tropical western Pacific, are noted for their large size.

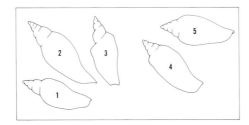

PLATE 110

[1] *Fulgoraria rupestris* Gmelin   4 to 5″

Fairly common in the East China Sea, this deep-water volute has wavy black markings on a light-brown ground.

[2] *Scaphella kieneri* Clench   4 to 9″

Endemic to the Gulf of Mexico, *Scaphella kieneri* is a rather rare deep-water volute. This specimen was taken off the coast near Biloxi, Mississippi.

[3] *Fulgoraria concinna* Broderip   4 to 5″

This species is found at a depth of 250 to 600 feet off the Pacific coast of Japan.

[4 and 5] *Scaphella junonia* Shaw   4 to 6″
Juno's Volute

One of the most highly prized shells native to American waters. It is found from North Carolina southward around Florida and into the Gulf of Mexico.

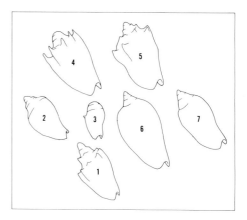

PLATE 111

[1] *Voluta pulchra* Sowerby   1½ to 2″

Voluta pulchra is native to the Great Barrier Reef, off Queensland, Australia.

[2] *Voluta nivosa* Lamarck   2 to 3″

This volute is found off the coast of northwest Australia.

[3 and 4] *Voluta imperialis* Lightfoot   6 to 10″
Philippine Imperial Volute

The smaller specimen is immature, and had been hatched recently from its egg case. The larger is also a juvenile, about two months old. The adult of this species attains a considerable size.

[5] *Voluta vespertilio* Linné   2 to 4″
Bat Volute

A common East Indian shell, the Bat Volute displays great variation in color, surface markings, and degree of spinal development.

[6 and 7] *Amoria undulata* Lamarck   2½ to 4″

This exquisitely marked volute is native to the waters off South Australia, New South Wales, and Tasmania. In general, the darker forms of this species are found in the more southerly part of its range.

PLATE 112 (*in color*)

[*top*] *Ericusa fulgetrum* Sowerby   4 to 5″
Lightning Volute

The Lightning Volute is a relatively rare shell native to shallow waters off South Australia.

[*Bottom left*] *Voluta studeri* von Martens   1½ to 2½″

From waters off southern Queensland and northern New South Wales.

[*Bottom center*] *Cymbiola cymbiola* Gmelin
2½ to 3″

The province of this very rare volute is believed to be from Indonesia to southern India. Little is known of the shell because it has not been found since the eighteenth century. Formerly in the American Museum of Natural History in New York, this specimen is now part of the collection of the Academy of Natural Sciences of Philadelphia.

[*Bottom right*] *Voluta lapponica* Linné   2½ to 3½″

This volute is native to the waters of the Indian Ocean.

PLATE 113 (*in color*)

[*left*] *Voluta angulata* Swainson   4 to 6″
Angular Volute

The waters off Uruguay and southern Brazil are the home of the unusual Angular Volute.

[*right, group of five*] *Amoria zebra* Leach   1 to 2″
Zebra Volute

The color and markings of the shells of this species show great variations, according to their exact habitat along the east coast of Australia.

PLATE 114 (*in color*)

Aulica aulica Lightfoot   3½ to 6″
Court Volute

The southern Philippines is the home of this rare species. Court Volutes vary greatly in structure and in surface projections, and their color ranges from a pale orange to the deepest red.

PLATE 115 (*in color*)

[*top*] *Iredalina aurantia* Powell   4 to 5″
Golden Volute

Although there are more species of volutes from Australian waters than from anywhere else in the world, there are comparatively few from New Zealand. One of these is the rare Golden Volute shown here.

[*bottom*] *Teramachia tibiaeformis* Kuroda   2½ to 3″
Shinbone Volute

A very rare deep-water volute from Japan.

PLATE 116

[*left*] *Voluta vespertilio* Linné   2 to 4″
Bat Volute

This specimen is an example of the occasional sinistral occurrence of a normally right-handed species (see plates 111, number 5, and 118, number 16).

[*right*] *Voluta peristicta* McMichael   2 to 3″

This small volute is from Queensland, Australia.

PLATE 117 (*in color*)

Volutoconus bednalli Brazier   3½ to 6″
Bednall's Volute

One of the rarest volutes known, this shell lives in deep waters off Northern Territory, Australia.

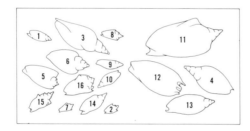

PLATE 118

[*1*] *Amoria damoni* Gray   3 to 4″
Damon's Volute

[*2*] *Voluta nivosa,* form *oblata* E. A. Smith   2 to 3″

Two species of volutes native to northwestern Australia.

[*3 and 4*] *Voluta sowerbyi* Kiener   5 to 8″

The two specimens show some of the possible variations in markings within the species. This volute is native to the waters between Australia and Tasmania.

[*5*] *Voluta hunteri* Iredale   4 to 7″

[*6*] *Voluta roadnightae* McCoy   5 to 8″

[*7*] *Voluta peristicta* McMichael   2 to 3″

[*8*] *Voluta wisemani* Brazier   2½ to 3″

[*9*] *Voluta sericata* Thornley   3 to 5″

[*10*] *Amoria maculata* Swainson   2 to 3″

[*11*] *Voluta magnifica* Gebauer   6 to 11″

[*12*] *Melo miltonis* Griffith and Pidgeon (not full-grown)   10 to 17″

[*13*] *Voluta papillosa* Swainson   5 to 6″

A group of volutes found in the waters off southern and eastern Australia.

[*14*] *Voluta swainsoni* Marwick   4 to 7″

[*15*] *Voluta arabica* Gmelin   4 to 5″

Two species from New Zealand: *Voluta swainsoni* is found off South Island, and *Voluta arabica*, off North Island.

[*16*] *Voluta vespertilio* Linné   2 to 4″
Bat Volute

PLATE 119

[*left*] *Voluta musica* Linné   2½ to 3½″
Music Volute

The Music Volute is found in the southern Caribbean and along the north coast of Venezuela. A great favorite with collectors, its varied decorations form designs that resemble musical staves and notes.

[*center*] *Voluta ebraea* Linné   4 to 5″
Hebrew Volute

The Hebrew Volute is found off the coast of Brazil.

[*right*] *Voluta nobilis* Lightfoot   3 to 5″
Noble Volute

This very heavy, uncommon member of the volute family is native to the waters surrounding the Malay Peninsula.

PLATE 120 (*in color*)
[*left top*] *Voluta flavicans* Gmelin   2 to 4″
Yellow Volute

This specimen was taken in deep water off Darwin, Australia. It ranges from northern Australia to New Guinea. A strongly formed, massive shell, it varies in color from bluish white to deep yellow.

[*left bottom*] *Voluta norrisi* Sowerby   2 to 3″

The specimen shown here was taken at a depth of 35 feet off Manus Island, New Guinea.

[*right*] *Voluta deshayesi* Reeve   3 to 4″
Deshayes' Volute

Deshayes' Volute is native to the waters around New Caledonia.

PLATE 121 (*in color*)
[*left*] *Volutoconus grossi* Iredale   4 to 6″
Gross's Volute

Volutoconus grossi is native to deep water off Queensland, Australia.

[*right top*] *Amoria turneri* Gray
Turner's Volute

This species is found off the north coast of Australia; the specimen shown here is from the Arafura Sea.

[*right bottom*] *Amoria canaliculata* McCoy
Channeled Volute

The Channeled Volute is found along the coast of Queensland, Australia. It is now moderately common, although formerly it was rare and brought high prices at auctions.

PLATE 122
[*left*] *Melo aethiopicus* Linné   6 to 14″
Ethiopian Volute

This species belongs to the group commonly known as bailer shells because they were used by natives for bailing out their boats. It is found throughout the tropical western Pacific. This specimen has been cut to show its subtly curved interior convolutions.

[*right*] *Voluta (Livonia) mammilla* Sowerby   8 to 10″

A southern Australian bailer shell characterized by its bulbous protoconch, the whorl at its apex.

PLATES 123, 124, and 125
Cymbium cymbium Linné   8 to 14″
False Elephant's Snout Volute

This unusual form of the False Elephant's Snout is seen from three angles. This species, noted for its uniquely shaped protoconch, is found off the western coast of Africa.

PLATE 126
Melo amphora Lightfoot   6 to 18″

Probably the largest of all bailer shells, *Melo amphora* is native to the waters off northern Australia The series shown here follows its growth from the immature to the full-grown specimen.

119

122

124

CONIDAE

Although the some five hundred species of cones are found all over the world in tropical seas, the majority come from the Indo-Pacific. Heavy and solid, the cone shells are noted for their magnificent marking and coloration, and certain species are among the rarest of all shells. Some of the larger Indo-Pacific cones can inflict extremely serious (at times fatal) stings. From its proboscis, the mollusk ejects poison via a harpoon-like stinger, which stabs the victim.

PLATE 127 (*in color*)
Conus textile Linné   2 to 4″
Textile, or Cloth of Gold, Cone

Textile cones are found mainly in the Indo-Pacific region. Their common name probably stems from the markings, which are reminiscent of certain Oriental brocades or flame-stitch fabrics. This is one of the largest of the venomous cones.

PLATE 128 (*in color*)
[*left top*] *Conus sozoni* Bartsch   2 to 4″
Sozon's Cone

Conus sozoni is an uncommon cone from Florida, the West Indies, and the Gulf of Mexico.

[*left bottom*] *Conus janus* Hwass   2 to 2½″

Conus janus, from the Indian Ocean, is considered quite rare. This specimen comes from Mauritius.

[*right*] *Conus* (species unknown)   2″

This interesting shell was taken off Noumea, on the southwest coast of New Caledonia, by the scuba diver and shell enthusiast Dr. Yves Merlet.

PLATE 129 (*in color*)
Conus bullatus Linné   2 to 3″
Bubble Cone

Most of the rare Conidae are virtually unobtainable, and the few known specimens are housed in museums. *Conus bullatus* is very rare, but fine examples come on the market from time to time. Its porcelaneous surface makes it unique among members of its family. It is native to the western Pacific.

PLATE 130 (*in color*)
[*left*] *Conus spurius* Gmelin   1½ to 2½″
Alphabet Cone

A rare variety of the common Alphabet Cone, from the east coast of Central America and southern Mexico.

[*center*] *Conus dominicanus* Hwass   1 to 3″
Incomparable Cone

Some shells not described as rare are still very difficult to obtain. *Conus dominicanus,* the prized *Conus cedo-nulli* of the eighteenth century, is one of these. Edgar Allan Poe, in the *Conchologist's First Book,* decries the high prices being paid at that time for shells. As an example, he mentions that *Conus dominicanus* sold for three hundred guineas. Recently, a limited number of specimens have been collected off some of the islands of the Lesser Antilles. The shell shown here is in the collection of the Academy of Natural Sciences of Philadelphia.

[*right*] *Conus pertusus* Hwass   1 to 1½″
Pertusa Cone

Conus pertusus is native to the Indo-Pacific, and is found as far east as Hawaii.

PLATE 131 (*in color*)

Conus milneedwardsi Jousseaume   3 to 7″
Glory of India Cone

One of the rarest of all cones, this species was formerly known as *Conus clytospirus*. This specimen was taken by the French trawler "Gambas" in 900 feet of water off the city of Mozambique on the east coast of Africa in 1965.

PLATE 132 (*in color*)

(with mirror image)

[*left*] *Conus adamsoni* Broderip   2″
Rhododendron Cone

This beautiful specimen of the rare central-Pacific Rhododendron Cone is in the collection of the Academy of Natural Sciences of Philadelphia.

[*right*] *Conus ichinoseana* Kuroda   1½ to 2½″
Ichinose Cone

From very deep waters off the Pacific coast of Japan.

PLATE 133

Conus marmoreus Linné   3 to 5″
Marble Cone

The Marble Cone is easily identified by its white or sometimes pinkish pyramid-shaped spots on a very dark background. Rembrandt made a lovely etching of this shell in 1650 (figure 12). The specimens shown here come from Bohol Island in the central Philippines; the species is common throughout much of the Indo-Pacific.

PLATE 134

Conus aulicus Linné   3 to 6″
Aulicus Cone

Conus aulicus, closely related to the Textile Cone, is probably also deadly poisonous to man. A relatively rare Indo-Pacific shell, it is shown here both with (left) and without (right) its outer skin.

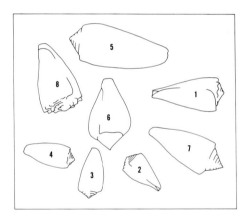

PLATE 135 (*in color*)

[*1*] *Conus nicobaricus* Hwass   2 to 4″

[*2*] *Conus miles* Linné (immature specimen)
2 to 3½″
Soldier Cone

[*3*] *Conus striatellus* Link (immature specimen)
3 to 5″

[*4*] *Conus geographus* Linné (immature specimen)
4 to 5″
Geography Cone

[5] *Conus episcopus* Hwass   2 to 3½″
[6] *Conus retifer* Menke   1½ to 2″
Netted Cone

These cones are all native to the Indo-Pacific.

[7] *Conus telatus* Reeve   1½ to 2″

A rare shell of the textile group, from the southern Philippines.

[8] *Conus marmoreus* Linné, form *vidua* Reeve
2 to 3″

An unusual form of the Marble Cone (plate 133), endemic to Philippine waters.

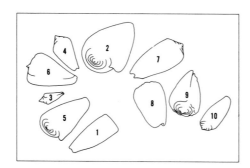

PLATE 136 (*in color*)
[1] *Conus nobilis* Linné   1 to 2″
Nobility Cone

A relatively rare shell from the southwestern Pacific, with a habitat apparently reaching from the Sulu Sea to the north coast of Borneo.

[2] *Conus suratensis* Hwass   2½ to 3″

A western Pacific shell.

[3] *Conus dispar* Sowerby   ¾ to 1″

A rare shell from the deep waters of the Gulf of California.

[4] *Conus ximenes* Gray   2″
Interrupted Cone

A western American shell with a range from the Gulf of California to Panama and southward.

[5] *Conus planorbis* Born   1½ to 3″
[6] *Conus eburneus* Hwass   1½ to 2″
Scotch Cone
[7] *Conus stercusmuscarum* Linné   1½ to 2″
[8] *Conus arenatus* Hwass   1 to 2″
[9] *Conus pulicarius* Hwass   1½ to 2″
[10] *Conus nussatella* Linné   2 to 3″
Nussatella Cone

Cones found throughout the Indo-Pacific region.

PLATE 137 (*in color*)
[*left*] *Conus zonatus* Hwass   1½ to 2½″
Zoned Cone

A rare shell, *Conus zonatus* is native to the northeast Indian Ocean, in the area of the Andaman Islands.

[*center top*] *Conus dalli* Stearns   1½ to 2½″
Dall's Cone

Dall's Cone is one of the many species related to the Textile Cone. It is native to the west coast of the Americas, from Lower California to Panama and the Galapagos Islands.

[*right top*] *Conus sowerbyi* Reeve 1 to 1½"
Sowerby's Cone

Conus sowerbyi is native to the Philippines. This specimen is from the Sulu Sea.

[*center bottom*] *Conus circumactus* Iredale 1 to 2"

An Indo-Pacific shell, this specimen was taken off Zamboanga, in the southern Philippines.

[*right bottom*] *Conus scalaris* Valenciennes 1½ to 1½ to 2" Ladder Cone

Native to the west coast of Mexico, *Conus scalaris* is found at a depth of 500 to 1,000 feet.

PLATE 138 (*in color*)

[*left*] *Conus litteratus* Linné 3 to 5"
Lettered Cone

The plentiful *Conus litteratus* is found throughout most areas of the Indo-Pacific. It has been a popular shell among Western collectors since the first specimens were brought to Europe in the sixteenth century. The specimen shown here is unusual in that it is dominated by dark colors.

[*right*] *Conus mustelinus* Hwass 3"
Mustelline Cone

The uncommon Indo-Pacific *Conus mustelinus* resembles the well-known *Conus capitaneus* but is distinctive because of its two rows of brown spots.

PLATE 139 (*in color*)

Conus genuanus Linné (enlarged detail) 1½ to 2"
Genua Cone

The rare *Conus genuanus* is indigenous to the coast of tropical western Africa. Its dots and dashes stand out on alternating wide and narrow white bands, which are set on a still wider banded surface of brown and mauve.

PLATE 140 (*in color*)

[*left*] *Conus tessulatus* Born 1 to 2"
Tessellate Cone

The markings on the *Conus tessulatus* vary not only in size and shape but also in color, from pale orange to deep crimson. The shell has a wide distribution in the Indo-Pacific.

[*center*] *Conus generalis* Linné 2½ to 3½"
General Cone

The high spire is typical of *Conus generalis*. This fairly common species is found throughout most of the Indo-Pacific area; the specimen shown here is from Cebu Island, in the Philippines.

[*right*] *Conus ammiralis* Linné 2 to 3"
Admiral Cone

Although found in widespread locations throughout the Indo-Pacific, the Admiral Cone is uncommon. This specimen comes from Jolo Island, in the Philippines.

PLATE 141 (*in color*)

Conus gloriamaris Chemnitz 4 to 5"
Glory-of-the-Seas

Although not the rarest of all shells, Glory-of-the-Seas has long been considered the most valuable (at auctions, it now brings prices exceeding one thousand dollars). Romantic legends have sprung up about it and its collectors, and include tales of pride, thievery, death, and destruction. Some seventy specimens are now extant, most of them housed in public museums. They come from various locations in the southwest Pacific, the Solomon Islands, New Guinea, Indonesia, and the Philippines. This specimen is number twenty-eight.

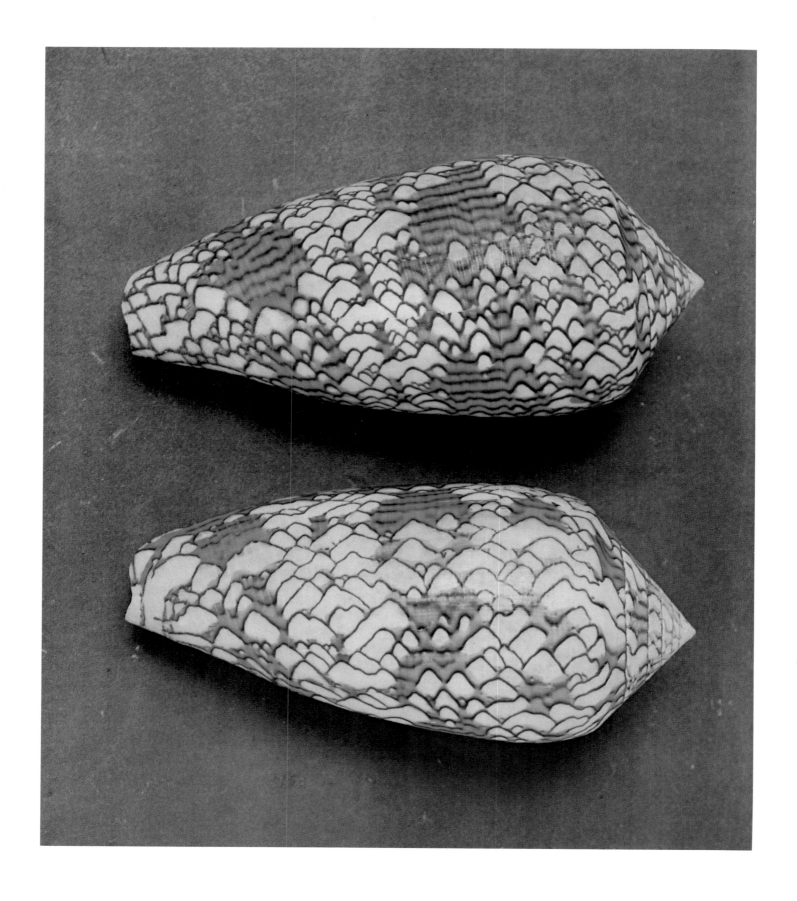

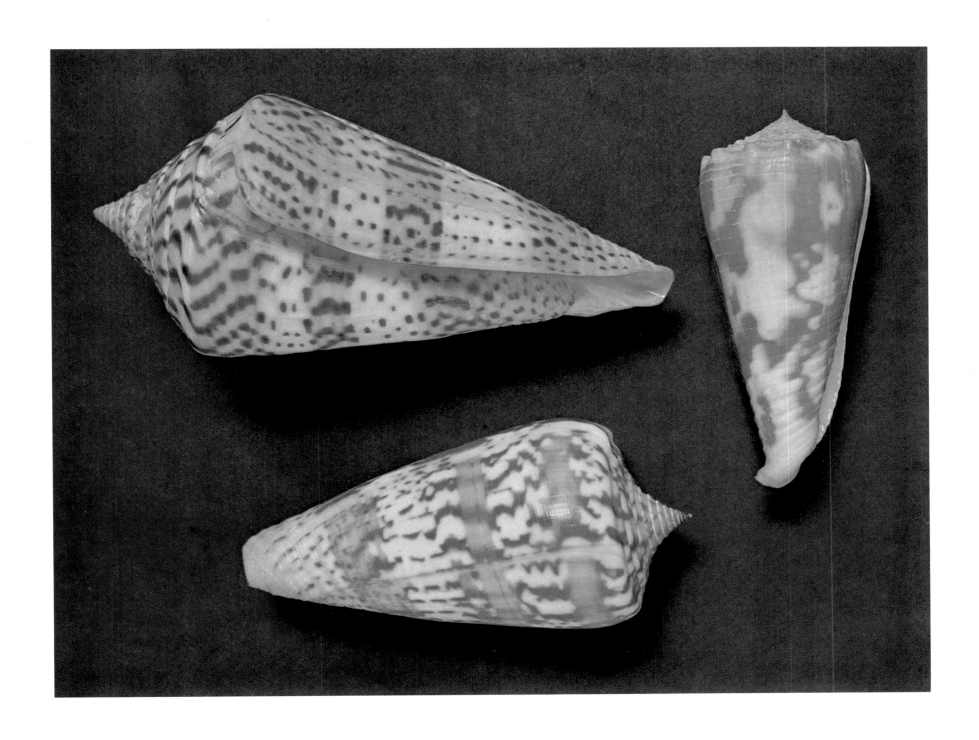

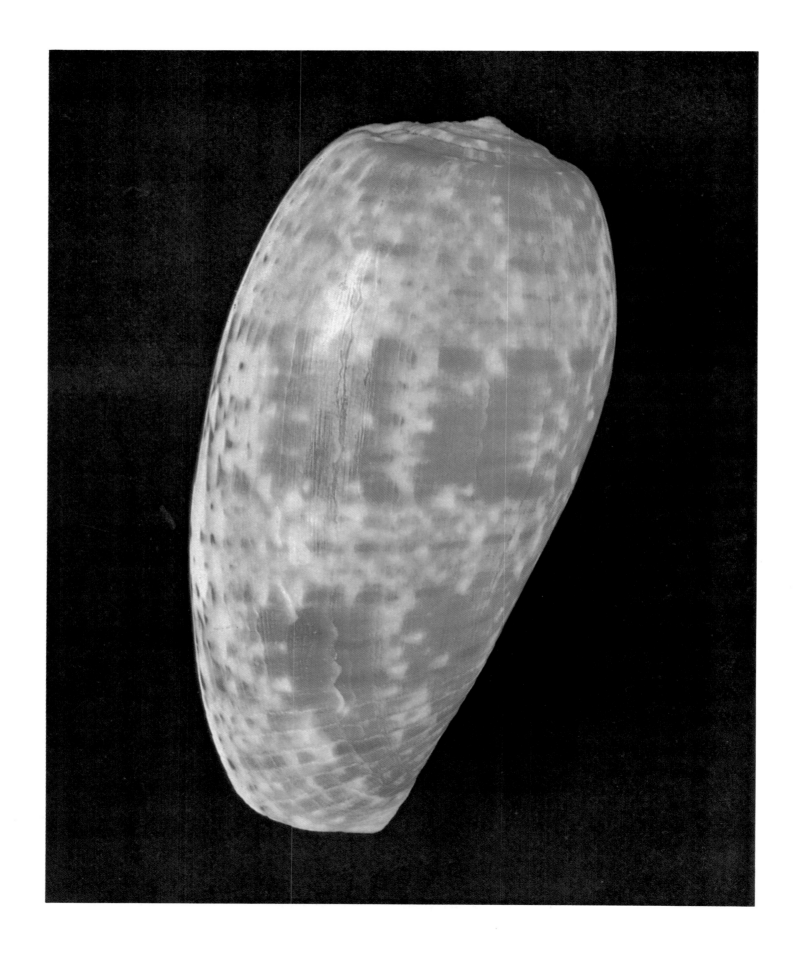

131

133

138

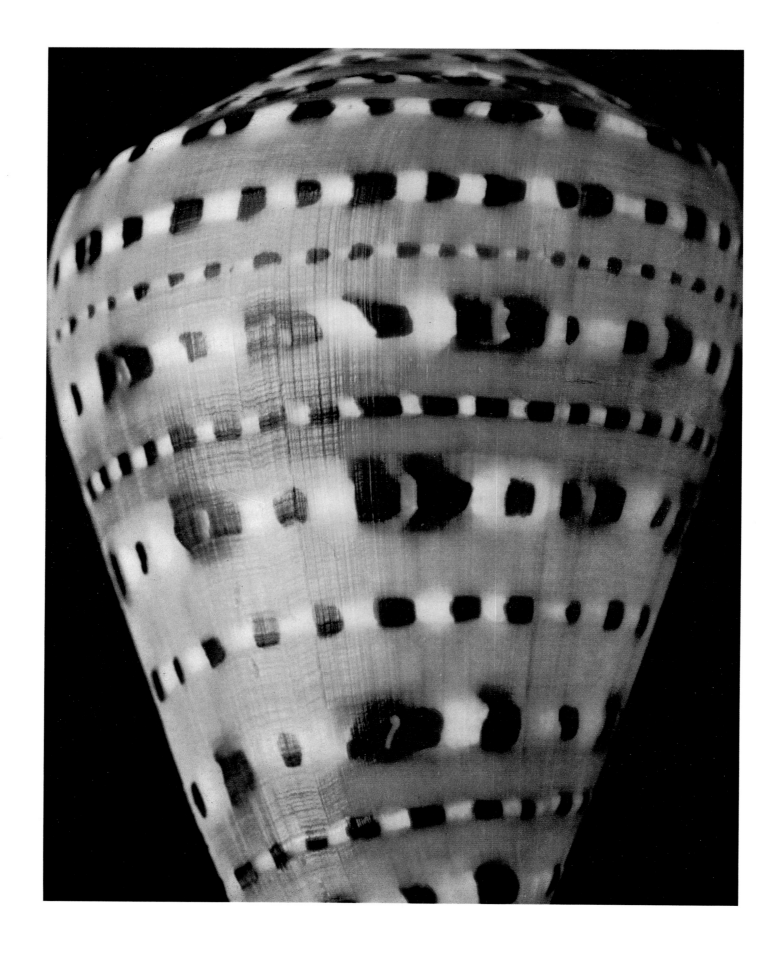

141

TEREBRIDAE

The Terebridae are known as auger shells because of their long, drill-like shape. Most of the three hundred species live in the sand in shallow, tropical waters.

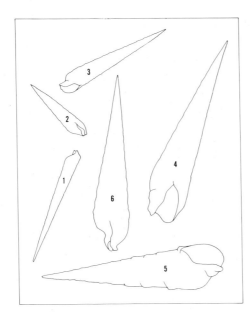

PLATE 142 (*in color*)

[*1*] *Terebra praelongas* Deshayes   2 to 3″

This small, brown shell with delicate surface decoration comes from northeast Australia.

[*2*] *Terebra lanceata* Linné   2″
Lance Auger

[*3*] *Terebra pretiosa* Reeve   3 to 4″

[*4*] *Terebra dimidiata* Linné   4 to 6″
Dimidiate Auger

[*5*] *Terebra crenulata* Linné   4 to 6″
Crenulate Auger

Several species of auger shells native to the Indo-Pacific.

[*6*] *Terebra taurinus* Lightfoot   4 to 6″
Flame Auger

A rare species, with flame-like markings, native to southern Florida, the Gulf of Mexico, and the Caribbean.

PLATE 143

[*two large shells*] *Terebra triseriata* Gray   3 to 5″
Triple-banded Auger

The Indo-Pacific is the home of this extremely

elongated species, a highly prized collector's item.

[*two small shells*] *Terebra praelongas* Deshayes
2 to 3″

TURRIDAE

The turrid shells comprise a large and variable world-wide family. Most of the species are no longer than three inches and have a deep indentation or notch on the upper part of the lip.

PLATE 144
[*from left to right*]
Turris crispa Lamarck   2 to 3″
Turris babylonia Linné   2 to 3″
Gemmula cosmoi Sykes   2 to 2½″
Lophiotoma indica Röding   2 to 3″

The notched lip, typical of this family, may readily be seen in these Indo-Pacific turrid shells.

PLATE 145
[*seven large shells*] *Thatcheria mirabilis* Sowerby
3 to 5″
Miraculous Thatcher Shell

Thatcheria mirabilis lives in deep water (400 to 600 feet) off the south coasts of the Japanese islands of Honshu and Shikoku. It is the world's largest turrid shell.

[*two small shells at right*] *Ancistrosyrinx pulcherrissimus* Kira   1½ to 2″

This small shell is native to the deep waters off Japan.

HYDATINIDAE and BULLIDAE

PLATE 146 (*in color*)
Shells of these families, usually known as bubble shells, are mostly from tropical waters.

[*top, group of three*] *Hydatina albocincta* van der Hoeven   1″
White-banded Bubble

An uncommon shell native to Japanese waters.

[*bottom left*] *Hydatina physis* Linné   1 to 2″
Paper Bubble

The shallow-water *Hydatina physis* of the Indo-Pacific is commonly found in eelgrass beds.

[bottom right, group of three] *Bullina nobilis* Habe ¾ to 1″
Noble Bubble

This red and white shell is found in deep waters off southern Japan and farther to the south.

ARCIDAE

Of the two hundred species of ark shells, twenty-four are native to the Americas. They are mostly tropical shells with a long, straight multitoothed hinge.

PLATE 147
Trisidos tortuosa Linné   3 to 4″
Twisted Ark Shell

Trisidos tortuosa, from the western Pacific, has a peculiar twisted shape which gives it a form unique among ark shells.

PLATE 148
Anadara philippiana Dunbar   2½ to 4″

Plainly visible in this photograph is the typical toothed hinge of the ark shells. This species is found in the Indian Ocean.

PTERIIDAE

PLATE 149 (*in color*)
Pteria penguin Röding   7″
Giant Wing Oyster

This fairly common Indo-Pacific wing oyster has a fragile, pearly shell. A specimen with a large pearl attached is a prized showpiece for any collection. The pearl has no great value in itself, but, because it is attached, increases the value of the shell.

ISOGNOMONIDAE

PLATES 150 and 151
Malleus albus Lamarck (immature specimen, 3 to 4″)
White Hammer Oyster

Malleus malleus Linné   4 to 9″
Hammer Oyster

The hammer oysters are found in the Indo-Pacific. Their common name comes from the obvious resemblance of the closed shells to hammers. (The shells are shown both open and shut.) The larger shell, *Malleus malleus,* has a purplish black exterior and a nacreous interior. *Malleus albus* has a white shell, which, when young, may be spotted (as is this specimen).

143

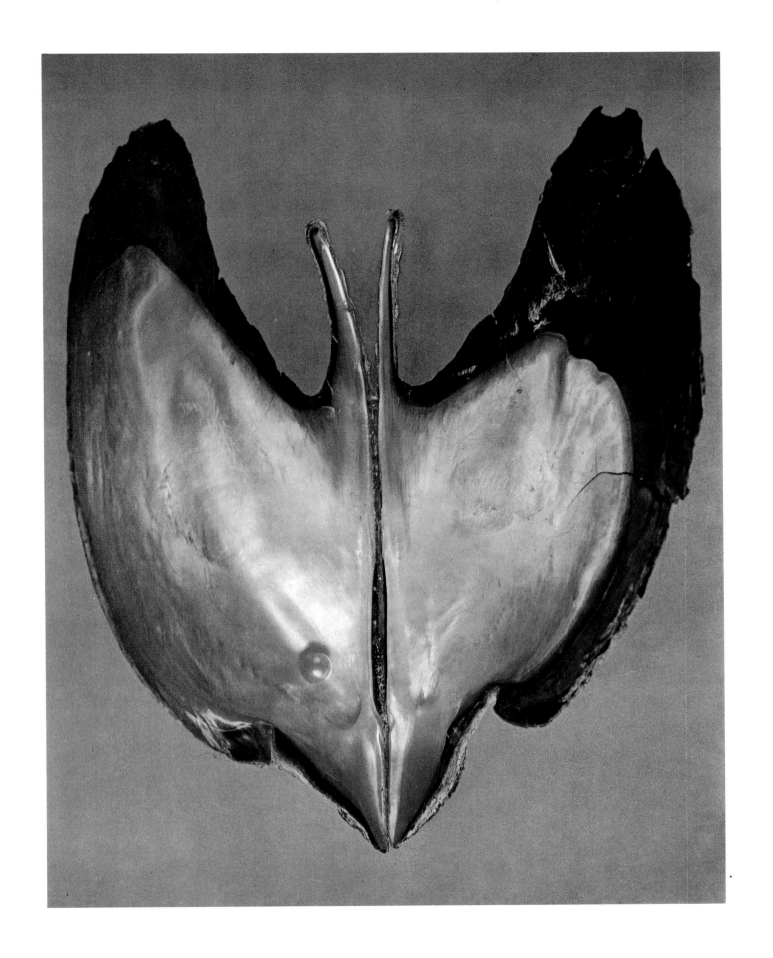

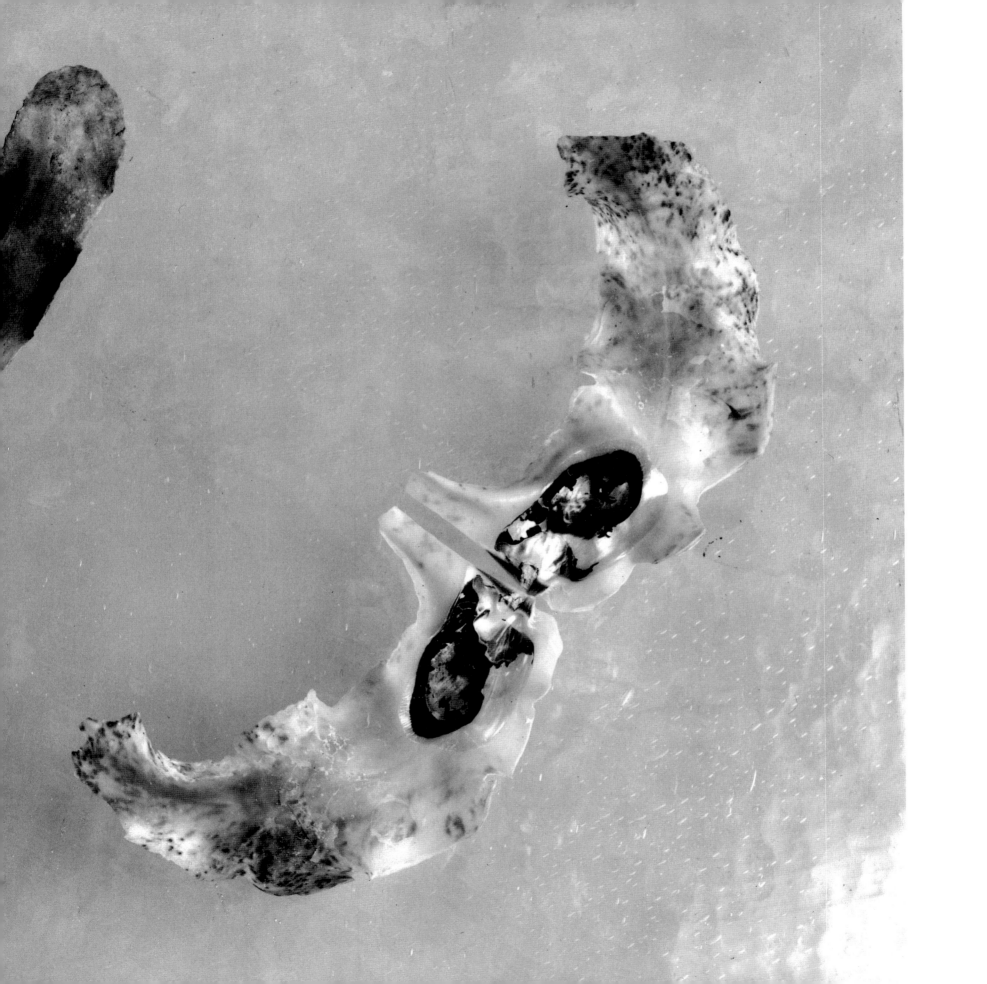

PECTINIDAE

Scallops are found throughout the world. They are among the most active bivalves, and move about rapidly by clapping their shell valves together. Most scallops have two convex valves, although some have one convex and one flat valve. The shells are characterized by radiating ribs, and often have bright colors; there are many color variations within the same species. The flesh of the cold-water scallop is edible.

PLATE 152 (*in color*)
Pecten gloriosus Reeve   1½ to 3″
Glorious Scallop

Common to Queensland and northeast Australian waters, *Pecten gloriosus* is a favorite with collectors because of its wide range of delicate colors.

PLATE 153
Pecten puncticulatus Dunker   3″

This Japanese scallop has one convex and one concave valve, one nesting inside the other.

PLATE 154 (*in color*)
[*top left*] *Pecten ziczac* Linné   2 to 4″
Sharp-turn Scallop

A fairly common scallop, *Pecten ziczac* is found off the south Atlantic coast of the United States and into the West Indies. The orange form shown here is quite rare.

[*top, center and right*] *Chlamys sentis* Reeve
1 to 1½″
Sentis Scallop

These small shells live under coral formations in approximately the same waters as *Pecten ziczac*. They have a wide variation of colors.

[*bottom*] *Pecten diegensis*   3 to 4″
San Diego Scallop

   Pecten diegensis lives in moderately deep water and is native to the coast of southern California.

PLATE 155 (*in color*) and PLATE 156
Lyropecten nodosus Linné   3 to 6″
Lion's Paw

   The Lion's Paw is native to many parts of the West Indies and to the coastal waters of the southeastern United States.

PLATE 157 (*in color*)
[*left*] *Pecten nobilis* Reeve   3 to 5″
Noble Scallop

   One of the most popular scallops among collectors is the deep-purple variety of *Pecten nobilis*, which is endemic to the waters off Japan.

[*center*] *Pecten gloriosus* Reeve   1½ to 3″
Glorious Scallop

[*right*] *Pecten australis* Sowerby   3 to 4″
Australian Scallop

   This yellow specimen of *Pecten australis* is from off Carnarvon in northwest Australia.

SPONDYLIDAE

The Spondylidae are commonly called chrysanthemum shells or thorny oysters. Their valves are attached by a unique type of ball-and-socket hinge, and the surface of the shells is covered with jagged, slightly curved spines of varying lengths. The shell lives attached to coral ledges and submerged wrecks.

PLATE 158
Spondylus wrightianus Crosse   5 to 6″
Wright's Chrysanthemum Oyster

This pure-white thorny oyster, shown here twice actual size, is native to Australian waters. Although the shell itself is relatively small, its elongated spines give it a total breadth of up to six inches.

PLATES 159 and 160 (*in color*)
Spondylus americanus Hermann   4 to 8″
American Chrysanthemum Shell

A species native to the waters off Florida and the West Indies. The characteristic hinge is visible in plate 160. The unusual occurrence of these shells growing attached to each other is seen in plate 159.

PLACUNIDAE

PLATE 161 (*in color*) and PLATE 162
Placuna sella Gmelin   5 to 10″
Saddle Oyster

Both the broad arch (saddle) of the exterior and the nacreous interior of this tropical shell may be seen in these photographs. The Saddle Oyster is native to shallow waters in the western Pacific.

153

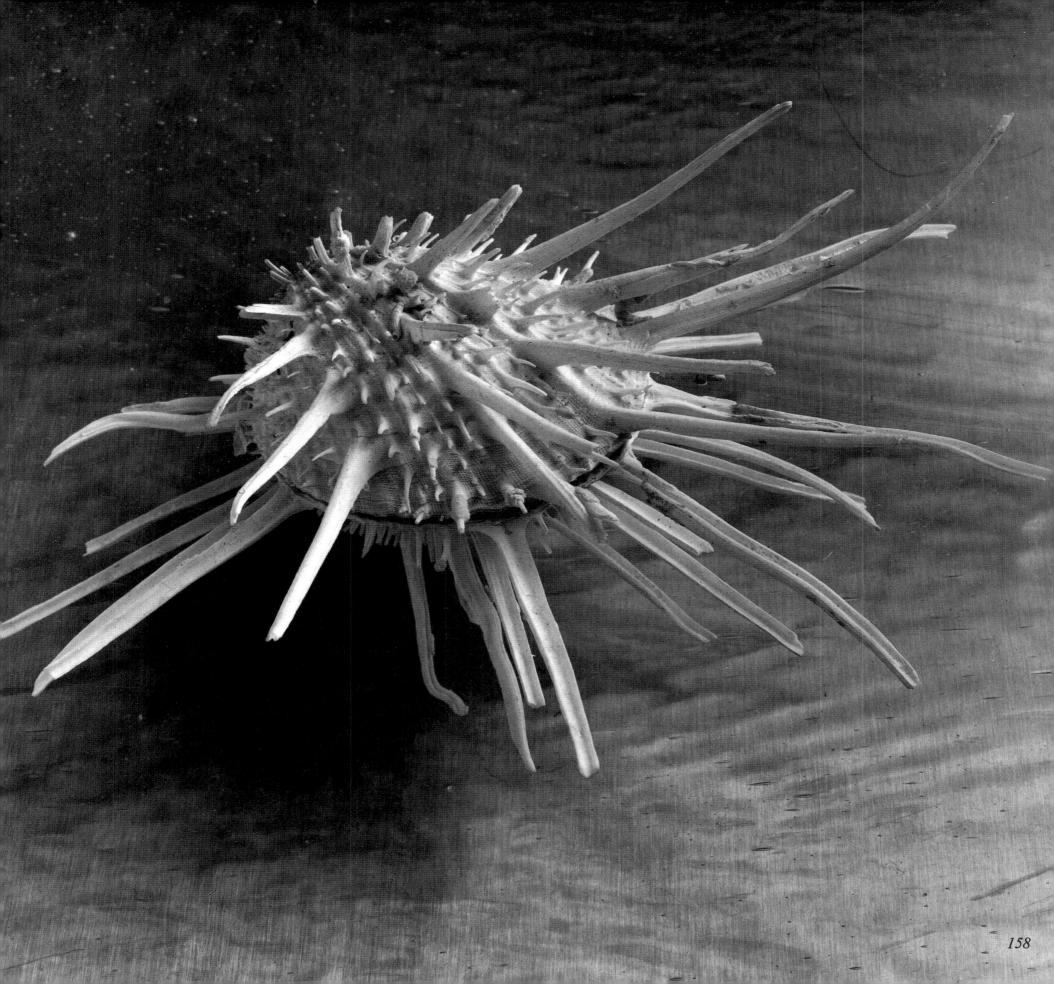

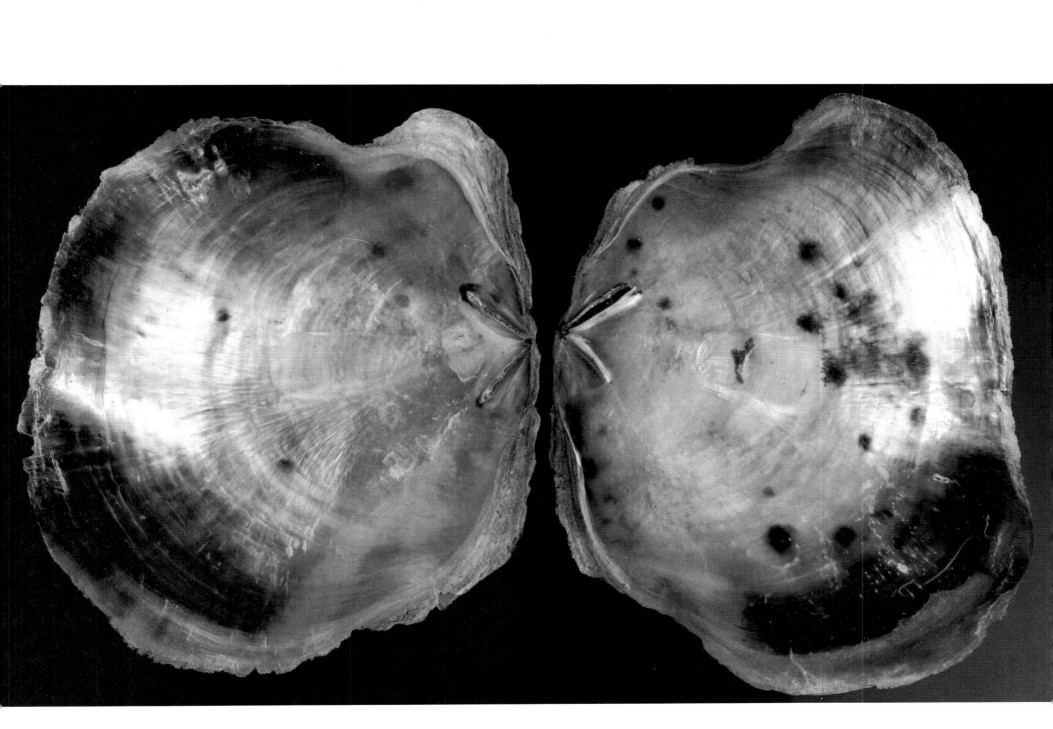

OSTREIDAE

PLATES 163 and 164 (*in color*)
Lopha cristagalli Linné   3 to 5″
Cock's Comb Oyster

　　True oysters (Ostreidae) are a rather small family of bivalves. They are usually found at the bottom of shallow water or clinging to rocks or other objects. Many oysters are gathered commercially for their edible flesh. *Lopha cristagalli i*s found in the tropical parts of the Indo-Pacific. Its characteristic edge can vary greatly: certain specimens may be quite regular, while others may show wildly haphazard angles. Its color may vary, also, from a pale slate-gray violet to a deep, dusty blue. Often, *Lopha cristagalli* is found in clusters attached to coral (plate 163).

TRIGONIIDAE

PLATE 165 (*in color*)
Neotrigonia margaritacea Lamarck (enlarged detail)
1 to 1½″

　　This unusual pearly bivalve is native to the waters off northern Tasmania and southeast Australia. A firm closure is assured by interlocking teeth of great precision.

TRIDACNIDAE

The Tridacnidae, or giant clams, include the largest shelled mollusks. The Giant Clam (*Tridacna gigas*) can reach up to four feet in length and weigh over five hundred pounds.

PLATE 166

Hippopus hippopus Linné   3 to 15″
Bear Paw Clam

　　The subtle variations in shape and markings of this clam are abundantly evident here. Notice the way both halves of the shell fit together and the beautiful interior configurations. The coloration of this species is a combination of whites, beiges, and brown tones.

The Bear Paw Clam is endemic to the waters from the Malay Peninsula to the Ryukyu Islands, Japan, and eastward as far as Samoa.

PLATE 167 (*in color*)
Tridacna squamosa Lamarck   4 to 16″

One of the most highly sculptured of all giant clams is *Tridacna squamosa,* widely distributed in the Indo-Pacific. Elongated, fluted scales, and varied pastel colors are characteristic of this species.

CHAMIDAE

PLATE 168
Chama lazarus Linné   3 to 4″
Lazarus Jewel Box

Jewel Boxes comprise about twenty species and vary greatly in form and color. They are tropical mollusks, found attached to rocks, coral, or wrecks. Their two valves are often of different sizes and shapes. The Lazarus Jewel Box is perhaps the most elaborate of these shells and is native to the Indo-Pacific.

CARDITIDAE

PLATE 169 (*in color*)
Cardita crassicostata Lamarck   2 to 3″
Rosy Cardita

Carditas, of which some thirty species exist, are found throughout the world in tropical waters. The Rosy Cardita is native to the western Pacific, from the southern Philippines to Australia. It is found with many different colorations.

CARDIIDAE

Cockles comprise a large group of colorful bivalves with a wide range of ribbed surface patterning. Like the scallops, they are quite active and can jump several inches by the aid of their muscular foot. Many of the cockles are edible.

PLATE 170

[left] *Cardium aculeatum* Linné   2 to 3″

This specimen of *Cardium aculeatum* is from the Bay of Naples; the shell is found throughout most of the Mediterranean.

[right] *Trachycardium consors* Sowerby   2 to 3″

Trachycardium consors is found off the west coast of the Americas fom the Gulf of California to Ecuador.

PLATE 171 (*in color*)

[left] *Glossus humanus* Linné   2 to 4″
Ox Heart

This edible cockle is found throughout the Mediterranean and along the Atlantic coast of North Africa, Spain, and Portugal. It was formerly called *Isocardia cor*.

[right] *Cardium beckei* Reeve   1½ to 2½″

A beautiful shell in both color and surface decoration, *Cardium beckei* is native to tropical western-Pacific waters and as far north as southern Japan.

PLATE 172

Glossus humanus Linné   2 to 4″
Ox Heart

PLATES 173 and 174

Cardium costatum Linné   4 to 5″
Costate Cockle

Several views of this deeply ribbed cockle from tropical west-African waters.

PLATE 175 (*in color*)

Corculum cardissa Linné   1 to 3″
Heart Cockle

The Indo-Pacific *Corculum cardissa* is a common shell. Most specimens are white or off-white; those tinted in pastel hues are rare. Some authorities assign different species to those with varying surface features. All the shells, however, have approximately the same distribution. The specimens shown here come from the central Philippines.

166

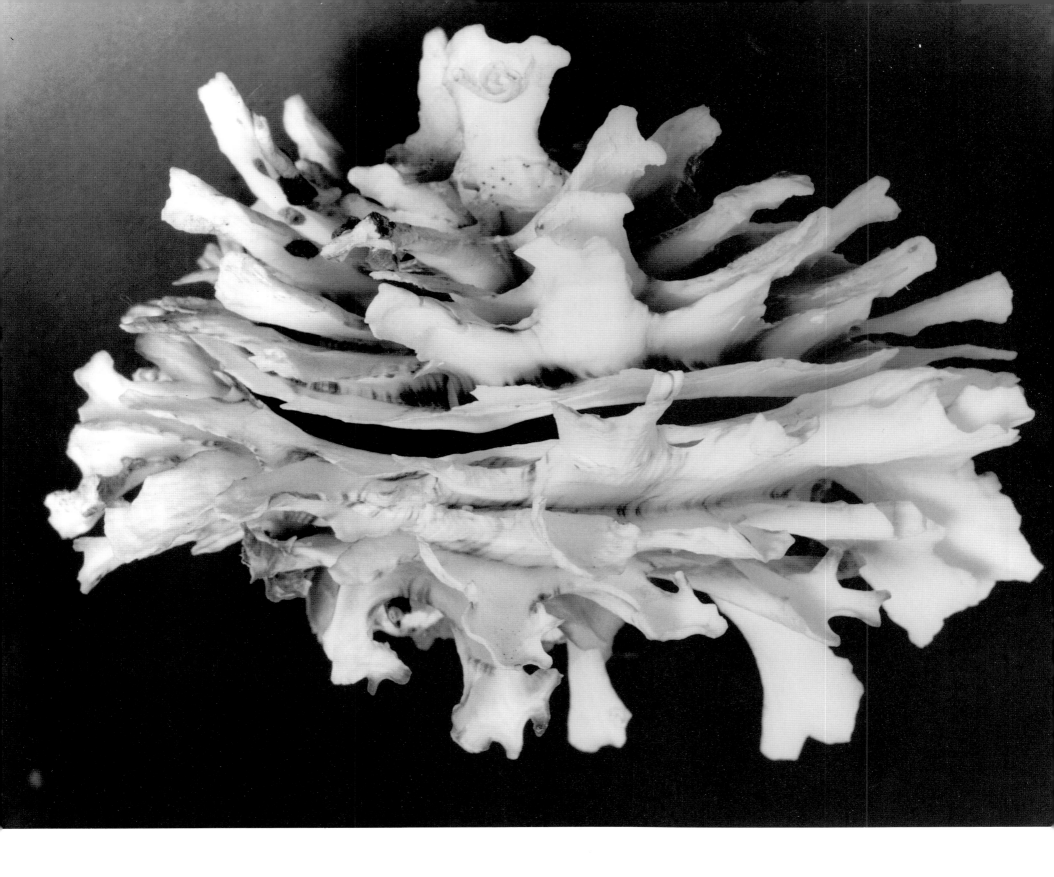

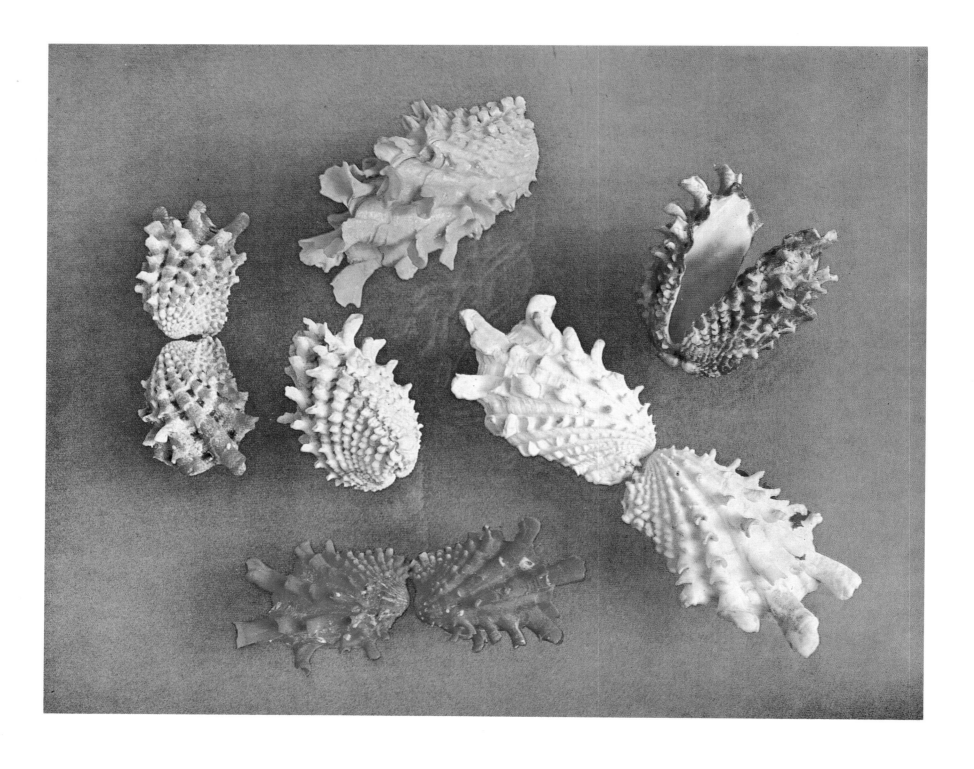

171

172

174

VENERIDAE

There are over four hundred species of Venus clams found all over the world. They include both the plain, edible clams, such as the Quahog of the eastern United States (marketed in its young stage as Cherrystone or Littleneck clams) and the more uncommon, elaborately designed species.

PLATE 176
Pitar lupinaria Lesson   1 to 2″
Pacific Comb Venus

This fantastic Venus clam is native to the west coast of the Americas from the Gulf of California to Peru.

PLATE 177
Callanaitis disjecta Perry   1 to 2½″
Wedding Cake Venus

The Wedding Cake Venus is unique in its surface sculpture. It is native to Australian waters, where it is found below the tide line on the sandy mud banks along the coast of New South Wales and Victoria.

PLATE 178
Tapes litterata Linné   4 to 5″
Lettered Venus

These marked clams come from the shores of Dirk Hartog Island off Western Australia. They are a much larger and sturdier variety of the common Pacific Lettered Venus (plate 181, number 2).

PLATE 179
Venus rosalina Rang   2½ to 4″
Leafy Venus

This deeply sculptured clam is found in tropic waters off western Africa.

PLATE 180
Lioconcha castrensis Linné   1 to 1½″

This cream-yellow clam, shown here greatly enlarged, is marked with a variety of angular blackish lines. It is common to many areas of the Indo-Pacific.

PLATE 181 (*in color*)
[*1*] *Paphia undulata* Born   1½ to 2″

This Venus clam has a shiny porcelaneous surface, patterned with a series of intersecting brown lines on a pale-beige ground. An Indo-Pacific clam, it is commonly found on muddy bottoms in bays. The specimen illustrated here comes from the Persian Gulf.

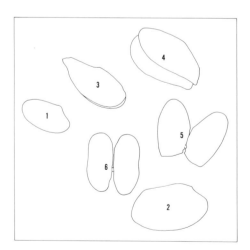

[2] *Tapes litterata* Linné   2 to 4″
Lettered Venus

A common Indo-Pacific shell, the Lettered Venus sometimes has purplish-brown markings instead of the more usual brown of this specimen.

TELLINIDAE

[3] *Tellina perrieri* Bertin   2 to 3″
[4] *Tellina variegata* Linné   2 to 3″
[5] *Tellina foliacea* Linné   1½ to 3″

The tellins are a colorful, fragile-shelled family of clams which live in the sand. They are native to the Indo-Pacific. *Tellina perrieri* is usually patterned with pinkish or reddish striations, like the one shown here. Rarely, a white specimen may be found. *Tellina foliacea,* a common shell, is characterized by its bright yellow tint. *Tellina variegata* is notable for its pale, fanlike vertical rays that intersect the brown-and-white striations that follow the contours of its shape.

SOLENIDAE

[6] *Siliqua radiata* Linné   1½″

The Solenidae, known commonly as the jackknife clams, dig more than a foot into the sand by means of their powerful foot. This shell is endemic to the Indo-Pacific.

LUCINIDAE

PLATE 182

Fimbria soverbii Reeve   2 to 4"
Elegant Fimbria Clam

The rare Elegant Fimbria is marked with delicate pink-tinted rays, and is sculpted with softly undulating ridges. It is found in the southwest Pacific.

PETRICOLIDAE

PLATE 183

[*top*] *Petricola pholadiformis* Lamarck   1½ to 2"
False Angel Wing

This tiny shell dwells on the tidal flats along the eastern coast of the United States and into the Gulf of Mexico.

PHOLADIDAE

[*bottom*] *Cyrtopleura costata* Linné   4 to 8"
Angel Wing

Angel Wing, also a mud dweller, is found on the eastern coast of the United States from New Jersey southward, and its habitat extends to the West Indies.

CLAVAGELLIDAE

PLATE 184

Penicillus penis Linné   4 to 6"
Watering Pot

This shell is a bivalve, although this is not apparent on first glance. The small bivalved shell from which it evolves is visible on the upper left of the horizontal specimen. This species lives buried in mud or sand in the Indo-Pacific. It is called Watering Pot because the perforated rounded end will sprinkle when the shell is filled with water.

NAUTILIDAE

PLATE 185 (*in color*)

Nautilus pompilius Linné   4 to 8"
Chambered Nautilus

Nautilidae are cephalopods; they swim over the ocean bottom in search of food and live in the outer chamber of their multichambered shell (see plate 186). Here, a juvenile shell of the famed Chambered Nautilus is shown against the background of a mature specimen. This species is native to the tropical western Pacific.

PLATE 186
Nautilus pompilius Linné   4 to 8″
Chambered Nautilus

A center slice of the shell clearly shows remnants of the siphonal canal, which pierces the series of gas-filled chambers used by this mollusk in balancing itself as it roams the ocean depths.

ARGONAUTIDAE

PLATE 187
[*left and bottom right*] *Argonauta nodosa* Lightfoot
3 to 8″
Paper Nautilus

[*top right*] *Argonauta hians* Lightfoot   2 to 3½″
Brown Paper Nautilus

The argonaut resembles the octopus, and does not inhabit this "shell." Formed by the female argonaut, the thin, calciferous shell is a case which she constructs with special tentacles, and is used to contain her eggs, which incubate within it. Once the eggs have hatched, the shell serves no purpose. Argonauts are found throughout the world in warm seas.

CHITONIDAE

PLATE 188
Amicula stelleri Middendorff   6 to 12″
Giant Pacific Chiton

Chitons comprise a rather large family of rocky shore dwellers with a world-wide distribution. One of the largest is the Giant Pacific Chiton, which is found along the coasts of Japan and western North America from Alaska to California. Only the segmented shell plates of the animal are shown here.

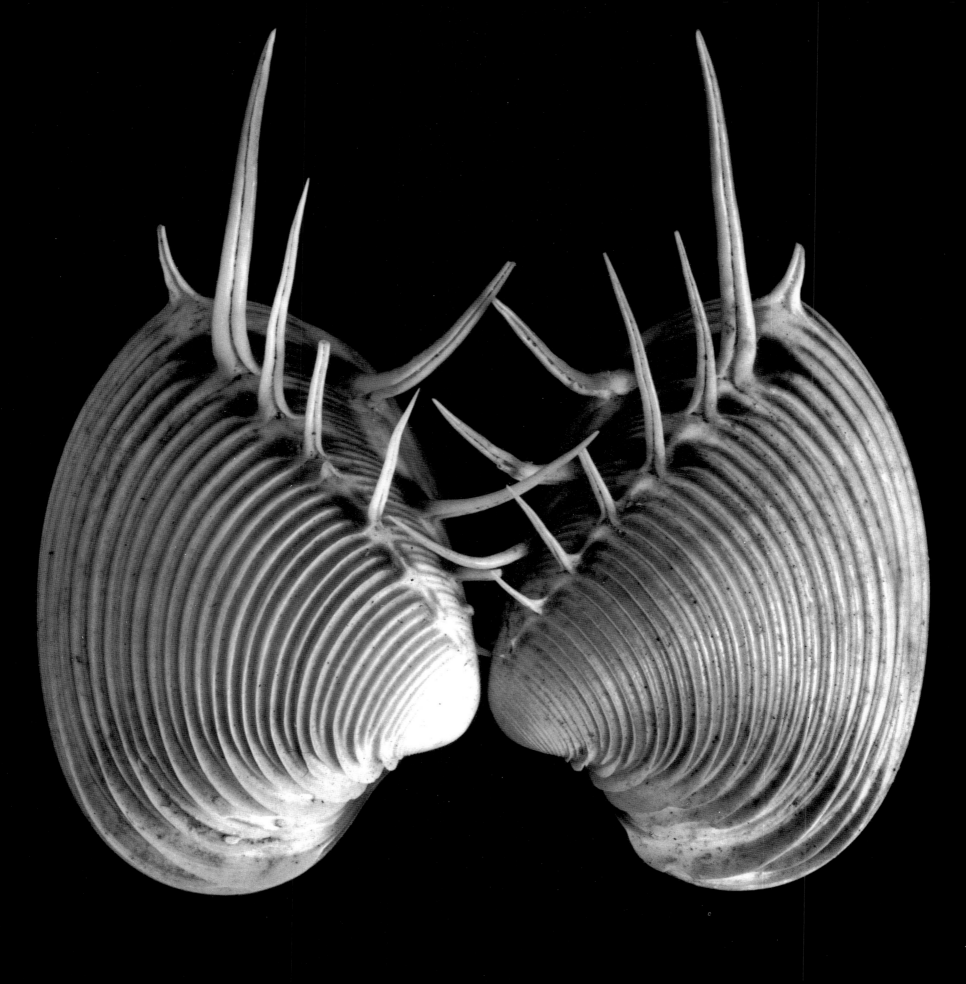

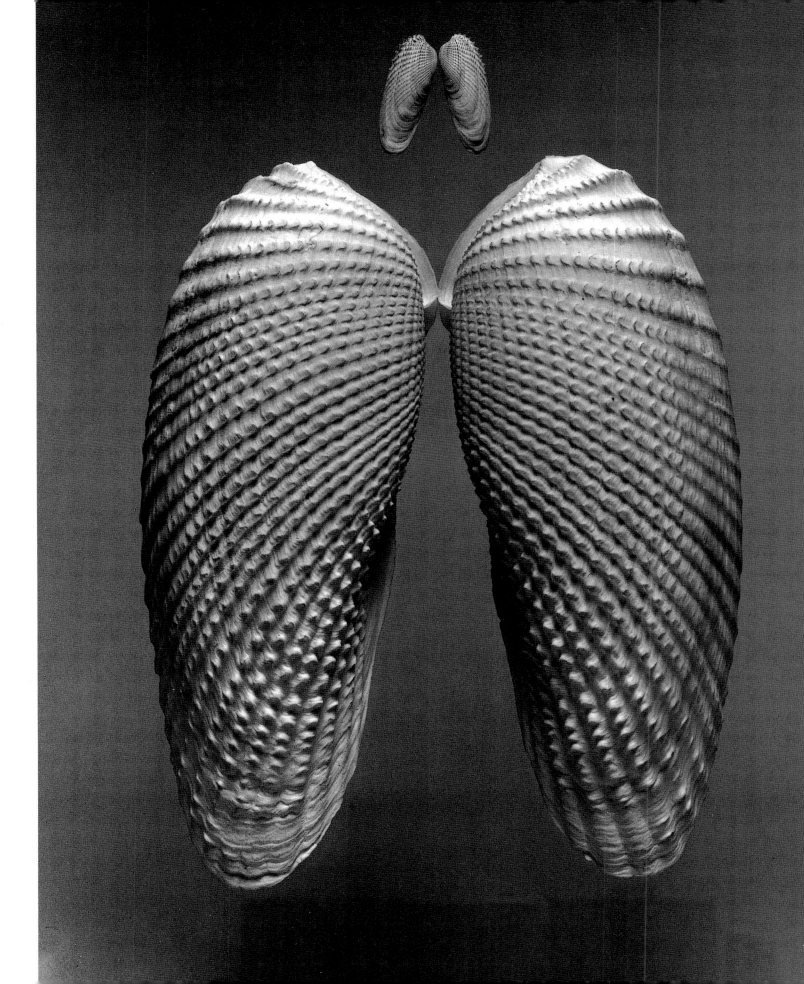

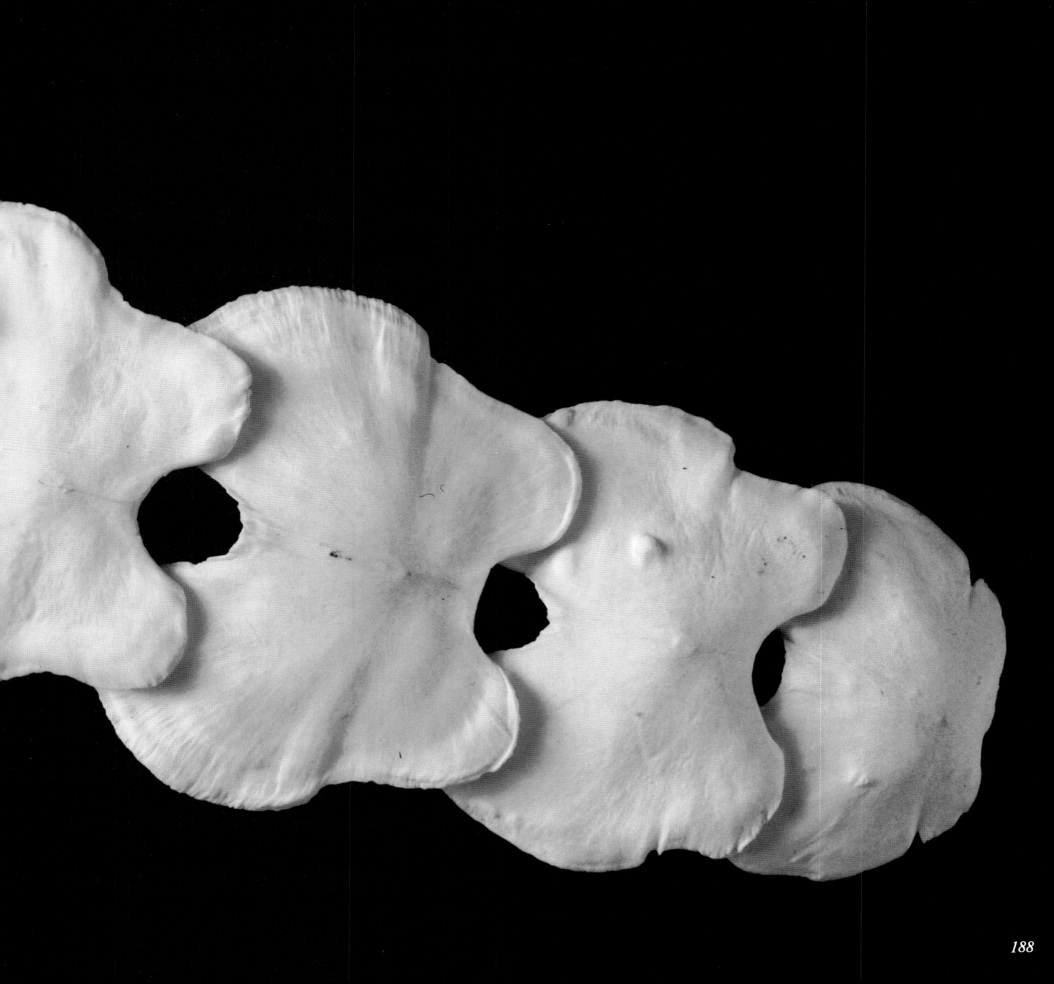

BIBLIOGRAPHY OF MARINE SHELLS
by R. Tucker Abbott, Ph.D.

Over 4,000 books and nearly 90,000 scientific articles have been published on the fascinating subject of shells and mollusks. We list here those we believe to be the most interesting, significant, and useful. They are arranged by subject matter, and give a glimpse into all phases of marine conchology.

ANTIQUITIES

322 B.C.

Aristotle. *History of Animals.* This great philosopher introduced the word "mollusk," dealt with their life habits and uses, and first proposed the names *Tellina, Nerita, Purpura,* and *Solen.*

77–79 A.D.

Pliny the Elder. *Natural History.* Tells how Royal Tyrian Purple dye was discovered and made from *Murex.*

1553

C. Gesner. *Icones Animalium quae in Historia Animalium.* A Swiss naturalist, who formed what was probably the first shell collection along scientific lines.

1681

P. Buonanni. *Ricreatione dell' occhio e della mente.* This Italian Jesuit priest wrote the first large book extolling the virtues of shell collecting, *Recreation for the Eyes and Mind.*

1685

Martin Lister. *Historia Conchyliorum.* A huge book, illustrated with woodcuts by his wife and daughter. Lister was physician to Queen Anne of England.

1742

A. J. D. Argenville. *L'Histoire Naturelle . . . la Conchyliologie.* This and subsequent editions revised by the conchologist Favanne were the main French texts of the 18th century.

1757

Michel Adanson. *Histoire Naturelle du Sénégal; Coquillages.* This is the first comprehensive study of the anatomy and life history of mollusks. It was far ahead of its time.

1758

Carolus Linnaeus. *Systema Naturae* (10th edition). Three hundred shells named. The beginning of the modern two-name system of nomenclature.

MONOGRAPHIC SERIES

1769–95

F. H. W. Martini and J. H. Chemnitz. *Neues systematisches Conchylien-Cabinet.* Nuremberg. 11 vols. The second series, 1837–1920, was continued by Küster, Kobelt, and others.

1816–22

M. de Lamarck. *Animaux sans Vertèbres.* Paris. Several un-illustrated volumes on mollusks.

1834–79

L. C. Keiner. *Spécies Général et Iconographie des Coquilles Vivantes.* Paris. 11 vols. A series of monographs with magnificently colored illustrations.

1842–87

G. B. Sowerby. *Thesaurus Conchyliorum, or Monographs of Genera of Shells.* London. 5 vols. Numerous small, hand-colored illustrations.

1843–78

Lovell A. Reeve and G. B. Sowerby. *Conchologia Iconica.* London. A 20-volume series of large, handsomely illustrated monographs.

1879–98

G. W. Tryon and H. A. Pilsbry. *Manual of Conchology* (marine series). Philadelphia. 17 vols.

1941–current

W. J. Clench (editor). *Johnsonia.* Monographs of the marine mollusks of the Atlantic by Clench, Turner, Abbott, Rosewater, and others. Harvard University Press, Cambridge, Mass. 4 vols.

1959–current

R. Tucker Abbott (editor). *Indo-Pacific Mollusca.* Monographs of the marine mollusks of the world with emphasis on the Indo-Pacific, by Abbott, Powell, Rosewater, and others. Colorplates. Academy of Natural Sciences of Philadelphia.

TEXTBOOKS OLD AND NEW

1825

H. M. de Blainville. *Manuel de Malacologie et de Conchyliologie*. Paris. The first of the so-called modern textbooks.

1850

G. Johnston. *An Introduction to Conchology*. London. An excellent account with well-documented historical notes.

1851

S. P. Woodward. *A Manual of the Mollusca*. London.

1853

R. A. Philippi. *Handbuch der Conchyliologie und Malacozoologie*. Halle. The first German textbook.

1859

J. C. Chenu. *Manuel de Conchyliologie et de Paléontologie Conchyliologique*. Paris. 2 vols.

1880

P. Fischer. *Manuel de Conchyliologie et Paléontologie Conchyliologique*. Paris.

1882

G. W. Tryon. *Structural and Systematic Conchology*. Philadelphia. 3 vols.

1895

A. H. Cooke. *Mollusca*. Volume 3 of the Cambridge Natural History Series. London.

1906

Paul Pelseneer. *Mollusca*. Volume 5 of *A Treatise on Zoology* (Edwin Ray Lankester, ed). London (Asher and Co., Amsterdam, 1964).

1929

J. Thiele. *Handbuch der systematischen Weichtierkunde*. Jena. 4 vols. A standard reference on classification.

1938

W. Wenz. *Handbuch der Paläozoologie: Gastropoda*. Volume 6 in 7 parts. Berlin. Gives modern higher classification.

1964

K. M. Wilbur and C. M. Yonge. *Physiology of Mollusca*. Academic Press, New York.

1967

L. H. Hyman. *The Invertebrates*, volume 6, *Mollusca I*. McGraw-Hill, New York.

POPULAR GENERAL CONCHOLOGY OLD AND NEW

1815

S. Brookes. *An Introduction to the Study of Conchology*. London. The first of many small 19th-century introductory books.

1821–34

W. Swainson. *Exotic Conchology*. London. A rare collection of 48 colorplates.

1839

Edgar Allan Poe. *The Conchologist's First Book*. Philadelphia. Second edition, 1843. (Poe wrote only the introduction.)

1851

Mary Roberts. *A Popular History of the Mollusca*. London. A charming and very informative introduction.

1908

Julia E. Rogers. *The Shell Book*. New York. This was the only good popular book available at the turn of the century.

1935

Walter F. Webb. *A Handbook for Shell Collectors*. Rochester, N. Y. The first dealer to publish a book with prices.

1955

R. Tucker Abbott. *Introducing Sea Shells*. D. Van Nostrand Co., Princeton, N. J.

1957

Kathleen Y. Johnstone. *Sea Treasure*. Houghton Mifflin Co., Boston. An excellent introduction to the hobby.

1958

F. Nordsieck. *Meeresschnecken*. Stuttgart. 44 plates of shell paintings.

1961

R. Cameron. *Shells*. London (Pleasures and Treasures series).

1966

R. T. Abbott (editor). *How to Collect Shells*. By various experts. Gives collecting techniques. Available for $2.00 from the American Malacological Union, Box 318, Route 2, Marinette, Wisconsin 54143.

1966

A. G. Melvin. *Sea Shells of the World*. Charles E. Tuttle, Rutland, Vermont. Lists prices.

1966

S. Peter Dance. *Shell Collecting*. Faber and Faber, London, and University of California Press, Berkeley. An excellent illustrated history of shell collecting.

1967

R. J. L. Wagner and R. T. Abbott. *Van Nostrand's Standard Catalog of Shells*. Lists thousands of shells and gives their approximate evaluations. Shell clubs and dealers listed. D. Van Nostrand Co., Princeton, N. J.

MODERN IDENTIFICATION BOOKS

WORLDWIDE

Abbott, R. Tucker. *Sea Shells of the World*. 1962. A Golden Nature Dollar Guide, New York.

Shikama, T. and Horikoshi, M. *Selected Shells of the World Illustrated in Colour*. 1963. Tokyo. 2 vols. Many beautiful colorplates.

THE AMERICAS

Abbott, R. Tucker. *American Seashells*. 1955. D. Van Nostrand Co., Princeton, N. J. 1,500 Pacific and Atlantic species.

Bousefield, E. L. *Canadian Atlantic Shells*. 1960. National Museum of Canada, Ottawa.

Keen, A. Myra. *Marine Shells of Tropical West America*. 1958. Stanford University Press, California.

———. *Marine Molluscan Genera of Western North America*. 1963. Stanford University Press, California. Illustrated keys.

Morris, P. A. *A Field Guide to the Shells*. 1951. Houghton Mifflin, Boston.

Warmke, G. L. and Abbott, R. T. *Caribbean Seashells*. 1961. Livingston Co., Narberth, Pennsylvania.

EUROPE

Arrecgros, J. *Coquillages Marins*. 1958. Libraire Payot, Lausanne.

Dautzenberg, P. *Des Coquilles des Côtes de France*. 1913. Bibliothèque de Poche du Naturaliste, no. 6. Paris.

Eales, N. B. *The Littoral Fauna of Great Britain*. 1929. Cambridge University Press.

Fretter, V. and Graham, A. *British Prosobranch Molluscs*. 1962. Ray Society, London.

Grimpe, G. and Wagler, E. (editors). *Tierwelt der Nord- und Ostsee*. Volume 9. Mollusk sections by Ankel, Boettger, Hoffman, Jutting, and Haas. Leipzig.

Nobre, A. *Moluscos Marinhos de Portugal*. 1932. Instituto Zoologia de Universidade do Pôrto.

Step, Edward. *Shell Life: An Introduction to the British Mollusca*. 1901. London. Despite its age, still worth reading.

Tebble, N. *British Bivalve Seashells*. 1966. British Museum (Natural History) Handbook, London.

AFRICA AND INDIA

Barnard, K. H. *A Beginner's Guide to South African Shells*. 1953. Maskew Miller, Cape Town.

Hornell, J. *Indian Mollusca*. 1951. Bombay Natural History Society.

Nickles, M. *Mollusques Testaces Marins de la Côte Occidentale d'Afrique*. 1950. Lechevalier, Paris.

Spry, J. F. *The Sea Shells of Dar-es-Salaam*. 1961. Tanganyika Society, Dar-es-Salaam.

JAPAN

Habe, T. *Shells of the Western Pacific in Color*. 1964. Volume 2. Hoikusha, Osaka.

Hirase, S. and Taki, I. *A Handbook of Illustrated Shells*. 1951. Maruzen, Tokyo.

Hirase, Y. *One Thousand Shells in Colour*. 1914–35. 4 vols. Unsodo, Kyoto. The famous accordion-pleated book with colored woodcuts. Only 400 complete sets made.

Kira, T. *Shells of the Western Pacific in Color*. 1965. Hoikusha, Osaka.

AUSTRALIA AND NEW ZEALAND

Allan, Joyce. *Australian Shells*. 1960. Georgian House, Melbourne.

Cotton, B. C. *South Australian Mollusca.* 1940–61. 3 vols. Government Printer, Adelaide.

McMichael, D. F. *Shells of the Australian Seashore.* 1960. Jacaranda Pocket Guide, Brisbane.

Macpherson, J. H. and Gabriel, C. J. *Marine Molluscs of Victoria.* 1962. National Museum of Victoria, Melbourne.

Powell, A. W. B. *Sea Shells of New Zealand.* Whitcombe and Tombs, Ltd., Auckland.

ART AND LITERATURE

Cox, Ian. *The Scallop.* 1957. Shell Transport and Trading Co., London. Studies of a shell and its influences on mankind.

Ehrhardt, A. *Muscheln und Schnecken.* 1941. Hamburg. A photographic study.

Hoare, Sarah. *Poems on Conchology and Botany.* 1831. London.

Jutting, Tera. *"Gloria Maris" Shells of the Malaysian Seas.* 1952. Amsterdam. A photographic study.

Krauss, H. K. *Shell Art.* 1965. Hearthside Press, New York.

Robert, P. A. *Kunstgebilde des Meeres.* 1936. Iris, Bern. 15 colored plates for framing.

Travers, L. A. *The Romance of Shells in Nature and Art.* 1962. M. Barrows, New York.

SPECIAL FAMILIES

Allan, Joyce. *Cowry Shells of World Seas.* 1960. Georgian House, Melbourne.

Lane, Frank W. *The Kingdom of the Octopus.* 1957. Sheridan House, New York.

Marsh, J. A. and Rippingale, O. H. *Cone Shells of the World.* 1964. Melbourne. Has 258 of the 500 known species.

Ranson, G. *La Vie des Huitres.* 1943. Librairie Gallimard, Paris.

Smith, Maxwell. *Review of the Volutidae.* 1942. Published by the author.

Yonge, C. M. *Oysters.* 1960. Collins, London.

CHILDREN'S BOOKS

Abbott, R. Tucker. *Quiz-Me: Seashells.* 1966. A Junior Golden Guide, Golden Press, New York. Inexpensive and informative.

Bevans, M. H. *The Book of Sea Shells.* 1961. Doubleday, Garden City, N. Y. Excellent for 10- to 15-year-olds.

Clemons, Elizabeth. *Shells Are Where You Find Them.* 1960. Alfred A. Knopf, New York.

Dudley, Ruth H. *Sea Shells.* 1953. Thomas Y. Crowell, New York.

Evans, Eva K. *The Adventure Book of Shells.* 1955. Golden Press, New York.

Hutchinson, W. M. *A Child's Book of Sea Shells.* 1954. Maxton, New York. Inexpensive and excellent.

Mayo, Eileen. *Shells and How They Live.* 1955. Pleiades Books, London.

Saunders, J. R. *A Golden Stamp Book of Sea Shells.* 1957. Golden Press, New York.

Tenney, Abby A. *Sea Shells and River Shells.* 1868. Boston. The first American children's book on shells.

GOURMET'S CONCHOLOGY

Anonymous. *How to Cook Oysters; How to Cook Clams; How to Cook Scallops.* 1953. 20 cents each from Superintendent of Documents, G.P.O., Washington, D. C. 20402.

Fisher, M. F. K. *Consider the Oyster.* 1941. Duell, Sloan and Pearce, New York. A superb collection of oyster recipes interlarded with a witty and informative text by one of America's finest writers on gastronomy.

Gaultier, Paul. "The Scallop at the Table," in *The Scallop.* 1957. Shell Transport and Trading Co., London.

Gibbons, Euell. *Stalking the Blue-eyed Scallop.* 1964. David McKay, New York. A delightful and useful shellfish cookbook; where to find and how to prepare shellfish.

Lovell, M. S. *The Edible Mollusks of Great Britain and Ireland, with Recipes for Cooking Them.* 1867. London. An informative, mouth-watering classic.

INDEX
OF ILLUSTRATED
SHELLS

Numbers in italics
refer to colorplates

Abalones 2
Acmaeidae 3
Admiral Cone *140*
Alphabet Cone *130*
Altivasum flindersi 106
American Chrysanthemum
    Shell *159, 160*
Amicula stelleri 188
Amoria
    canaliculata *121*
    damoni 118
    maculata 118
    turneri *121*
    undulata 111
    zebra *113*
Anadara philippiana 148
Ancillista velesiana *100*
Ancistrosyrinx
    pulcherrissimus 145
Angaria melanacantha 4, 5
Angel Wing 183
Angular Volute *113*
Architectonica perspectiva
    16, 17
Arcidae 147, 148
Argonauta
    hians 187
    nodosa 187
Astraea
    heliotropium 8, 9
    undosa 7, 8
Auger shells *142, 143*
Auger Turritella 14
Aulica aulica *114*
Aulicus Cone 134
Australian Scallop *157*
Australian Trumpet Shell
    95

Bailer shells 118, 122, 126
Barbados Keyhole Limpet
    3
Barnacle Rock Shell 84
Baryspira albocallosa *100*
Bat Volute 111, 116, 118
Bear Paw Clam 166
Bednall's Volute *117*
Belcher's Miter 101
Boivin's Cowrie *46*
Bonnet shells 48, 49
Brazilian False Olive *100*
Brown Paper Nautilus 187
Bubble Cone *129*
Bubble shells *146*
Buccinidae 92–96
Buccinum
    adelphicus 92
    tenuissimum 93, 94
Bullina nobilis *146*
Busycon
    candelabrum 92
    contrarium 92

Cabrit's Murex *61*
Callanaitis disjecta *177*
Cardiidae 170–75
Cardita crassicostata *169*
Cardium
    aculeatum 170
    beckei *171*
    costatum 173, 174
Caribbean Vase 105
Carnelian Cowrie *38*
Carrier shells 28–32
Casmaria erinaceus 48
Cassidae 47–49
Cassis
    cornuta 47
    fimbriata 49
    madagascariensis 48
    tuberosa 48
Cerithium fasciatum 18
Chama lazarus 168
Chambered Nautilus
    185, 186
Chank shell *107*

Channeled Volute *121*
Charonia tritonis 50, 51
Chestnut Cowrie *45*
Chickpea Cowrie *46*
Chiragra Spider Conch 25
Chitonidae 188
Chitons 188
Chlamys sentis *154*
Chrysanthemum shells
    158–60
Clavagellidae 184
Clavus Murex 78
Cloth of Gold Cone *127*
Cockles 170–75
Cock's Comb Oyster
    163, 164
Colorful Atlantic Natica
    33
Comb of Venus 59
Common Spider Conch
    25
Concholepas concholepas
    84
Conchs 22–25, 97
Cones 127–41
Conidae 127–41
Conus
    adamsoni 132
    ammiralis *140*
    arenatus *136*
    aulicus 134
    bullatus *129*
    circumactus *137*
    dalli *137*
    dispar *136*
    dominicanus *130*
    eburneus *136*
    episcopus *135*
    generalis *140*
    genuanus *139*
    geographus 135
    gloriamaris *141*
    ichinoseana *132*
    janus *128*
    litteratus *138*
    marmoreus 133
        form vidua *135*

miles 135
milneedwardsi *131*
mustelinus *138*
nicobaricus *135*
nobilis *136*
nussatella *136*
pertusus *130*
planorbis *136*
pulicarius *136*
retifer *135*
scalaris *137*
sowerbyi *137*
sozoni *128*
spurius *130*
stercusmuscarum *136*
striatellus *135*
suratensis *136*
telatus *135*
tessulatus *140*
textile *127*
ximenes *136*
zonatus *137*
Coralliophila pyriformis *90*
Corculum cardissa *175*
Costate Cockle 173, 174
Court Volute *114*
Cowries 36–46
Cox's Cowrie *46*
Crenulate Auger *142*
Cymatiidae 50–55
Cymatium spengleri 53, 54
Cymbiola cymbiola *112*
Cymbium cymbium
    123–25
Cypraea
    annettae *45*
    argus *38*
    asellus *46*
    aurantium *41*
    boivini *46*
    carneola *38*
    clandestina *46*
    coxeni *46*
        hesperina *36*
    cribraria *46*
    decipiens *38*
    depressa *45*

diluculum *46*
eburnea *45*
erosa *45*
felina fabula *45*
fimbriata *46*
friendii *44*
fultoni *37*
gracilis *46*
  japonica *46*
guttata *39*
helvola *46*
hesitata, *form* alba *40*
hirasei *37*
hirundo *46*
histrio *45*
isabella *45*
kieneri *46*
labrolineata *46*
lamarcki *45*
limacina *46*
lutea *46*
lynx *45*
mappa *40, 42, 43*
mauritiana *38*
moneta *41, 45*
nucleus *46*
onyx *38, 45*
pulchella *45*
pulchra *38*
punctata *36*
pyrum *38*
quadrimaculata *46*
saulae *36*
spadicea *45*
staphylaea *46*
stercoraria *38*
stolida *36*
subviridis *45*
sulcidentata *38*
talpa *45*
tessellata *44*
testudinaria *45*
thersites *38*
tigris *45*
turdus *45*
venusta *40*
verconis *46*

walkeri *45*
  bregeriana *36*
  ziczac *46*
  zonaria *45*
Cyrtopleura costata 183

Dall's Cone *137*
Damon's Volute 118
Decipiens Cowrie *38*
Deshayes' Volute *120*
Dimidiate Auger *142*
Distaff Spindle 98
Distorsio reticulata 52

Elegant Fimbria Clam 182
Emperor Helmet 48
Emperor's Slit Shell *1*
Endive Murex 74
Episcopal Miter *104*
Epitoniidae 20, 21
Epitonium
  magnificum 20
  scalare 20
  stigmaticum 20
Ericusa fulgetrum *112*
Eroded Cowrie *45*
Ethiopian Volute 122
Eyed Cowrie *38*

False Angel Wing 183
False Elephant's Snout
  Volute 123–25
Fasciolariidae 96–98
Fimbria soverbii 182
Fissurella
  barbadensis 3
  fascicularis 3
Flame Auger *142*
Florida Horse Conch 97
Forreria
  belcheri 81
  cerrosensis 82, 83
Friend's Cowrie *44*
Fulgoraria
  concinna 110
  rupestris 110
Fulton's Cowrie *37*

Fusinus
  colus 98
  eucosmius 98
Fusitriton oregonensis 55

Gemmula cosmoi 144
General Cone *140*
Genua Cone *139*
Geography Cone *135*
Giant clams 166, *167*
Giant Keyhole Limpet 3
Giant Pacific Chiton 188
Giant Wing Oyster *149*
Glorious Scallop *152, 157*
Glory of India Cone *131*
Glory-of-the-Seas *141*
Glossus humanus *171,* 172
Golden Cowrie *41*
Golden Volute *115*
Graceful Cowrie *46*
Gray Bonnet 49
Great Spotted Cowrie *39*
Green Abalone 2
Grinning Tun 56
Groove-Toothed Cowrie
  38
Gross's Volute *121*

Haliotis
  fulgens 2
  rufescens 2
Hammer Oyster 150, 151
Harp shells *108, 109*
Harpa
  costata *109*
  davidis *108*
  harpa *108*
Hawkwing Conch 23
Heart Cockle *175*
Hebrew Volute 119
Helmet shells 47, 48
Hemifusus morio 95
Hippopus hippopus 166
Histrio Cowrie *45*
Honey Cowrie *46*
Horned Helmet 47
Humpback Cowrie *38*

Hydatina
  albocincta *146*
  physis *146*

Ichinose Cone *132*
Imperial Delphinula 4, 5
Imperial Harp *109*
Incomparable Cone *130*
Interrupted Cone *136*
Iredalina aurantia *115*
Isabel Miter *101*
Isabelle Cowrie *45*
Isognomonidae 150, 151

Janthina janthina *19*
Japanese Carrier Shell
  28, *29, 30*
Jenneria pustulata *46*
Jewel Boxes 168
Juno's Volute 110

Kawamura's Latiaxis 89
Kiener's Cowrie *46*
King Helmet 48
Kinoshita's Latiaxis 88
Kira's Latiaxis 89

Ladder Cone *137*
Lady's Curl 15
Lamarck's Cowrie *45*
Lambis
  chiragra 25
  crocata 25
  lambis 25
  scorpius 25
  violacea 24
Lamp Chank *107*
Lance Auger *142*
Latiaxis
  deburghiae 89
  idoleum 87
  kawamurai 89
  kinoshitai 88
  kiranus 89
  lischkeanus 85, 86
  mawae 85, 86
  pilsbryi 88

spinosus *90*
tosanus 88
winckworthi 88
Lazarus Jewel Box 168
Leafy Purpura *79*
Leafy Venus 179
Left-handed Whelk,
   see Lightning Whelk
Lettered Cone *138*
Lettered Venus 178, *181*
Lightning Volute *112*
Lightning Whelk 92
Limpets 3
Lioconcha castrensis 180
Lion's Paw *155*, 156
Lischke's Latiaxis 85, 86
Little Donkey Cowrie *46*
Lobeck's Murex *58*
Lopha cristagalli *163, 164*
Lophiotoma indica 144
Lucinidae 182
Lynx Cowrie *45*
Lyropecten nodosus
   155, 156

Magilidae 85–91
Magnificent Wentletrap 20
Malea ringens 56
Malleus
   albus 150, 151
   malleus 150, 151
Map Cowrie *40, 42, 43*
Marble Cone 133
Martini's Tibia *26*
Mawe's Latiaxis 85, 86
Megathura crenulata 3
Melo
   aethiopicus 122
   amphora 126
   miltonis 118
Miraculous Thatcher Shell
   145
Miss de Burgh's Latiaxis
   89
Miter shells 101–4
Mitra
   belcheri 101

caffer, *form* formosensis
   103
clathrus 103
exasperata 103
filaris 103
glans 103
granatina 103
granosa 103
hirasei 103
isabella 101
mitra *104*
papilio 103
taeniata *102*
Mitridae 101–4
Mole Cowrie *45*
Money Cowrie *41, 45*
Murex
   alabaster *57*
   axicornis *70*
   beaui *71*
   bipinnatus *64*
   cabriti *61*
   cervicornis *63*
   cichoreus *74*
   cornucervi *57, 65–67, 69*
   elenensis *77*
   elongatus *78*
   haustellum *76*
   hirasei *75*
   lobeckii *58*
   macropterus *79*
   mindanensis *71*
   monodon, *see* Murex
     cornucervi
   nigritus *61*
   palmarosae *62*
   pecten *59*
   saulii *62*
   scorpio *68*
   senegalensis *77*
   sobrinus *77*
   stainforthi *76*
   steeriae *80*
   territus *72, 73*
   tripterus *64*
   triremus, *see* Murex
     pecten

tweedianus *75*
vespertilio *64*
zamboi *60*
Muricidae 57–84
Music Volute 119
Mustelline Cone *138*

Nassaria magnifica *97*
Naticidae 33
Nautilus pompilius
   185, 186
Neosimnia catalinensis *34*
Neotrigonia margaritacea
   165
Neptunea decemcostata
   92
Netted Cone *135*
New England Neptune 92
Nobility Cone *136*
Noble Bubble *146*
Noble Scallop *157*
Noble Volute 119
Noble Wentletrap 21
Nucleus Cowrie *46*
Nussatella Cone *136*

Oliva porphyria *99*
Olivancillaria urceus *100*
Olividae *99, 100*
Onion Tun 56
Onyx Cowrie *38, 45*
Opeatostoma pseudodon
   96
Orange Spider Conch 25
Ostreidae *163, 164*
Ovula ovum 35
Ovulidae *34, 35*
Ox Heart *171*, 172
Oysters 149–51, 158–64

Pacific Comb Venus 176
Pacific Triton 50, 51
Paper Bubble *146*
Paper Nautilus 187
Papery Rapa 91
Paphia undulata *181*
Patella mexicana 3

Pear Cowrie *38*
Pecten
   australis *157*
   diegensis *154*
   gloriosus *152, 157*
   nobilis *157*
   puncticulatus *153*
   ziczac *154*
Pectinidae 152–57
Penicillus penis 184
Perspective Sundial 16, 17
Pertusa Cone *130*
Petricola pholadiformis
   183
Petricolidae 183
Phalium
   bisulcatum 48
   glaucum 49
   granulatum 49
   strigatum 49
Phanozesta semitorta 50
Phasianella
   australis 12, 13
   ventricosa 12
Philippine Imperial Volute
   111
Pholadidae 183
Pilsbry's Latiaxis 88
Pink Conch 23
Pitar lupinaria 176
Placuna sella *161*, 162
Pleuroploca gigantea 97
Pleurotomaria hirasei *1*
Polinices mammilla 33
Powis' Tibia *26*
Precious Wentletrap 20
Pteria penguin *149*
Pterorytis foliata *79*
Punctate Cowrie *36*
Purple Sailor *19*
Pustularia cicercula *46*

Queen Conch 23
Queen Eugenia's Latiaxis
   87
Queen Helmet 48
Queen Tegula *6*

Rapa rapa 91
Rat Cowrie *38*
Red Abalone 2
Rhododendron Cone *132*
Robust Carrier Shell *31*
Rooster Conch *22*
Rose-branch Murex *62*
Rosy Cardita *169*

Saddle Oyster *161*, 162
San Diego Scallop *154*
Saul's Cowrie *36*
Saul's Murex *62*
Scaphella
  junonia 110
  kieneri 110
Scorpion Conch *25*
Scorpion Murex *68*
Scotch Bonnet 49
Scotch Cone *136*
Sentis Scallop *154*
Sharp-turn Scallop
  154
Shinbone Volute *115*
Shuttlecock *34*
Sieve Cowrie *46*
Siliqua radiata *181*
Snipe's Bill Murex 76
Soldier Cone *135*
Solenidae *181*
Sowerby's Cone *137*
Sozon's Cone *128*
Spider Conchs *24*, 25
Spindle shells 98
Spindle Tibia *26, 27*
Spinose Latiaxis *90*
Spondylus
  americanus *159, 160*
  wrightianus 158
Star shells 7–9
Sthenorytis pernobilis *21*
Stigmatic Wentletrap 20
Stolid Cowrie *36*
Striped Bonnet 49
Strombidae 22–27
Strombus
  canarium 23

gallus *22*
gigas 23
raninus 23
vittatus japonicus 23
Sundials 16, 17
Syrinx aruanus 95

Tapes litterata 178, *181*
Tapestry Turban *10*
Tegula regina *6*
Tellina
  foliacea *181*
  perrieri *181*
  variegata *181*
Tent Olive *99*
Teramachia tibiaeformis
  115
Terebellum terebellum 23
Terebra
  crenulata *142*
  dimidiata *142*
  lanceata *142*
  praelongas *142*, 143
  pretiosa *142*
  taurinus *142*
  triseriata 143
Tessellate Cone *140*
Tessellate Cowrie *44*
Textile Cone *127*
Thatcheria mirabilis 145
Thersite Cowrie *38*
Thorny oysters *158–60*
Thrush Cowrie *45*
Tibia
  fusus *26, 27*
  martinii *26*
  powisi *26*
Tiger Cowrie *45*
Tonna allium *56*
Tonnidae 56
Tortoise Cowrie *45*
Tosa Latiaxis 88
Trachycardium consors
  170
Tridacna squamosa *167*
Tridacnidae 166, *167*
Trigoniidae *165*

Triple-banded Auger 143
Trisidos tortuosa 147
Triton shells 50–55
Trivia radians *46*
Trochidae *6*
Tudicula armigera 105
Tulip shells 97
Tun shells 56
Turban shells *10, 11*
Turbinidae 7–13
Turbo
  fluctuosus *10, 11*
  petholatus *10*
Turner's Volute *121*
Turridae 144, 145
Turris
  babylonia 144
  crispa 144
Turritella terebra 14
Twisted Ark Shell 147

Umbilicate Cowrie *40*

Vasidae 105, 106
Vasum muricatum 105
Veneridae 176–81
Venus clams 176–81
Venus rosalina 179
Vermetidae 15
Vermicularia spirata 15
Violet Spider Conch *24*
Volema pugilina 95
Voluta
  angulata *113*
  arabica 118
  deshayesi *120*
  ebraea 119
  flavicans *120*
  hunteri 118
  imperialis 111
  lapponica *112*
  (Livonia) mammilla 122
  magnifica 118
  musica 119
  nivosa 111
    form oblata 118

nobilis 119
norrisi 120
papillosa 118
peristicta 116, 118
pulchra 111
roadnightae 118
sericata 118
sowerbyi 118
studeri *112*
swainsoni 118
vespertilio 111, 116, 118
wisemani 118
Volutidae 110–26
Volutoconus
  bednalli *117*
  grossi *121*
Volva
  birostris *34*
  brevirostris rosea *34*
  volva *34*

Walker's Cowrie *36, 45*
Watering Pot 184
Wedding Cake Venus 177
Wentletraps 20, 21
Whelks 92–95
White-banded Bubble *146*
White Hammer Oyster
  150, 151
Winckworth's Latiaxis 88
Wobbly Keyhole Limpet 3
Wright's Chrysanthemum
  Oyster 158

Xancus angulatus *107*
Xenophora
  exutus *32*
  pallidula 28, *29, 30*
  peroniana *32*
  robusta *31*
Xenophoridae 28–32

Yellow Volute *120*

Zebra Volute *113*
Zigzag Cowrie *46*
Zoned Cone *137*